The Art of Decorative
Mosaics

Elaine M. Goodwin

THE CROWOOD PRESS

Salutations: **To the Muse,**
Whoever She - or He - might be
EMG

First published in 1999 by
The Crowood Press Ltd
Ramsbury, Marlborough
Wiltshire SN8 2HR

Paperback edition 2008

British Library Cataloguing-in-Publication Data

A catalogue record for this book is available from the British Library.

ISBN 978 1 84797 056 5

Designed and edited by
Focus Publishing, Sevenoaks, Kent

Printed and bound in Singapore by Craft Print International

Contents

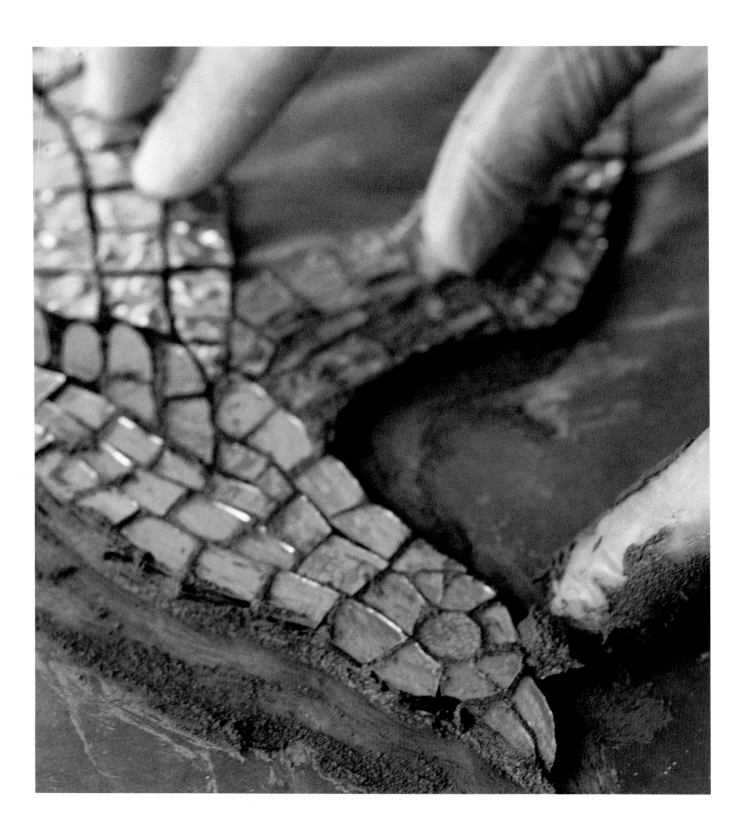

Acknowledgements

M y thanks to all who helped me realize this book: publishers and scholars, builders and artists from all ages, mosaic suppliers and mosaicist friends both here and abroad.

Warmest thanks to Lindy Ayubi who converted typewritten scraps into disk form with unflagging encouragement against many computer mischiefs. Grateful and delighted thanks to John Melville who tirelessly photographed work at all hours, in all weathers, to ensure the gleam in a piece of gold. My thanks as ever to Maurice Stapley for his practical expertise, and to Tony Wheaton for constructing the fountain, and special thanks to Bob Field for the geometric drawings. A hug for Antonia A.Wilson for putting the sparkle into the sundial, and a kiss for Darius Alexander for foregoing a few suppers along the way . . .

All the mosaics in the book were designed and created by the author, unless otherwise specified.

Introduction

Mosaic always has an enormous decorative appeal, whether it is a shimmering ceiling, a vividly coloured wall, or a highly geometric and detailed floor. The materials are in themselves hypnotically alluring: gold, glass, marble, semi-precious stones, even pebbles.

This book has two main objectives: firstly to instruct, and secondly to inspire in the art of mosaic making. Thus its primary objective is to teach the rudiments of mosaic making so that the reader will be able to make mosaics with total confidence and with a full working knowledge of materials, techniques and methods. These are all explained clearly and in detail, and the author has made unique mosaic panels to illustrate each material, each technique and each method of laying a mosaic.

Secondly the book aims to inspire in the reader a desire to create original works, and to give him or her the confidence to experiment with designs and techniques. An extensive and enlightening history of mosaic is given, from the earliest ventures in the art up to the present day, concentrating on the decorative elements so as to broaden the reader's knowledge of the art of mosaics still further, as well as to inspire creativity and aspiration.

Finally, extensive details of mosaic sites around the world, both historical and contemporary, are included, together with a glossary, a book list, and a list of stockists. The book also contains useful information about mosaic schools and workshops, and a selected gallery of the author's own work.

WHAT IS A MOSAIC?

No one is quite sure where the term 'mosaic' comes from – perhaps from the Muses: and although none of these nine goddesses is connected with the visual arts, the concept of the connection remains inspirational.

The term 'mosaic' can be defined as individual units with no particular identity, fixed together to form a whole with a unique and complete identity. What then is a mosaic? A mosaic is a decorative surface, fixed to a two- or three-dimensional base support. The mosaic can be placed, hung on a wall, fixed as a mural, a ceiling or a floor, or it can cover a free-standing or bas-relief object or sculpture. The decorated surface is made of hand-cut material of normally close tessellation. The spaces between each unit should be apparent on the surface, and are generally filled with mortar.

The cut pieces, which may be of any shape, are called *tesserae* (singular: *tessera*), a traditional term meaning 'cube', now used generically to cover all materials for mosaic use. These anonymous tesserae are stuck to a base support, using an adhesive, to make up a design which may be representative, abstract, illustrative or calligraphic. The tesserae, which may include a variety of materials such as: glass; stone; ceramic; marble and gold, may be used singly or collectively.

9

1 Setting up a Workspace

THE WORKSPACE

Mosaic making can be divided into three processes: design and drawing, making and fixing, and grouting. The first needs a clean surface area, the second a sound work surface, and the third an area impervious to cement mess. Ideally all three should be accommodated in one space: the mosaic workspace.

Whatever area of a room is chosen, it should be able to accommodate the making of smaller and larger pieces, with space for viewing the work as it progresses, and with a clearly defined drawing and making area. The work surfaces must be of such a height in relation to the seat or chair to give a comfortable working posture, as mosaic making often involves hours of concentration. Aware of this fact, the artist should take frequent breaks away from the work, and should be conscious of maintaining a relaxed posture whenever working.

The floor and other surfaces will frequently be covered in fragments of cut mosaic material, and it is good practice to sweep up or vacuum the area regularly to keep down the ever-accumulating shards of tesserae and dust. Sometimes such a sweep-up will reward by bringing to light a 'lost' piece, or the sweepings will yield precious fragments for further use, particularly when working in gold.

Lighting, whether it is artificial using tungsten or daylight bulbs, or natural light from a window, should be good and bright to facilitate more accurate cutting and detailed tessellation. Sometimes directional light may be needed as well, when a spotlight or an anglepoise lamp may be used. It is a good idea to position the main working area close to a window if work is to be carried out most frequently during daylight hours. Public works are often done outside *in situ*, in varying light conditions; and portable mosaics can be worked on outside in a garden or paved area so as to maximize light and ventilation.

SAFETY PRECAUTIONS

Safety precautions of a high standard should be observed when mosaic making, in order to avoid unnecessary accidents or damage, and protective clothing should be worn at all times. Eye shields or safety goggles should be worn whenever cutting mosaic material, as should dust masks or respirators to avoid the inhalation of dust. Rubber or vinyl gloves must be worn when working with cement, and when using hydrochloric acid or masonry cleaner equivalents. Many artists also wear protective clothing or overalls whilst working in the studio or workspace.

Good ventilation is of paramount importance when using epoxy resins or fixatives, spray paints or spray adhesives.

It is strongly recommended that the instructions on all products are read thoroughly before use, and that the most

Right. Storage: adjustable shelving and brackets.

stringent safety procedures are strictly observed throughout the entire process of mosaic making.

STORAGE

Much mosaic material is heavy, and glass jars, boxes or other containers of mosaic need sturdy shelves with easy access and identification. Sort the materials into type and colour, putting heavy pebbles or marble on the ground or on lower shelves. Even stored materials thus arranged can delight and stimulate merely by the observation of their colour and texture – all this before they are even used in a mosaic!

DRAWING IMPLEMENTS

Keep drawing implements and materials together near the clean design area so they are easily available. They will include pens, chalks, crayons, conté crayons, charcoal, rubbers, a ruler, a protractor, compasses, pencils, set squares, sharpeners, a Stanley knife and some 'Blutack'.

There should also be plenty of paper in a variety of types and sizes; this should include drawing, tracing and graph paper. And it may also be helpful to have books, posters, postcards and other inspirational material near at hand – anything which aids the Muse and initiates the creative process.

FIXING IMPLEMENTS

A mosaicist is a natural accumulator, particularly of utensils which help in the making of a work, and a collection of knives, spatulas, tweezers, dental tools, palette knives, brushes and prodders will be acquired to suit

individual needs. These can be kept close at hand to the main working area on a wheeled trolley or conveniently positioned table.

GROUTING AND CLEANING EQUIPMENT

Much of this equipment may be kept in a shed and stored outside, and will include buckets, bowls, cloths, trowels, squeegee and brushes. Many mosaicists prefer to grout outside, especially on larger and three-dimensional works, because there is more room and any mess is more easily cleaned up.

The process of cleaning a mosaic with dilute hydrochloric acid or a brand cement cleaner should always be performed outdoors with direct access to water and good drainage.

2 Cutting Tools

THE HAMMER AND HARDIE

A great number of tools used in mosaic making are general household items, such as hammers, felt-tipped pens, brushes, paper, buckets and plastic gloves. Specialist tools are those employed to cut into tesserae of varying size and thickness the wide range of materials chosen specifically to create mosaics.

Using the hammer and hardie
A hammer and hardie is the most ancient, and, with practice, the most accurate, tool for cutting traditional tesserae. To use it, hold the piece of material to be cut between the forefinger and thumb, and rest it on the cutting edge of the hardie in the direction of the required cut. Strike it with the hammer directly from above, onto and over the cutting edge. A quick, firm but light strike creates a clean cut without splintering the material. The hammer and hardie are indispensable for cutting marble, smalti, stones and small pebbles.

THE HAMMER (ITALIAN: *MARTELLINA*)

The hammer has a wooden handle and a curved, steel head; the latter has two cutting edges, often toughened with tungsten. Hammers come in differing weights and should be selected to suit the individual mosaicist. A typical weight would be between 800g and 1kg (1lb12oz and 2lb 2oz).

THE HARDIE (ITALIAN: *TAGLIOLO/A*)

This is used in conjunction with the hammer. It is like a stonemason's chisel in character, having an upper cutting edge but with a long pointed base which is embedded into a block of wood or a heavy log. Being portable, a block is sometimes found to be more versatile, since it can be set on a variety of working surfaces to suit a standing or a sitting position. Alternatively, a heavy log can be cut to exactly the right height for the individual mosaicist when seated: the log is then placed between the knees and gripped lightly during the cutting process.

MOSAIC NIPPERS

The mosaic nipper is a type of pincer which is most commonly used to cut manufactured glass, ceramic, china, gold, and, to a lesser extent, smalti. If held correctly, it can be used continuously for hours without causing the operator

Using the mosaic nippers
Hold the long legs of the mosaic nipper well down into the cutting hand for maximum leverage and control. Take the material to be cut between the thumb and forefinger, and insert it between the two cutting edges up to a depth of 6mm (¼ in).
For a perfect cut, simultaneously squeeze the legs of the nipper together in one hand while pressing the material in the other with an identical force or pressure.

Opposite page: At work with the hammer and hardie.

undue fatigue. The secret is in the spring which ensures that the cutting edges are always open, so that one cut can follow another immediately. The cutting edges are tipped with tungsten carbide to give a highly durable sharp edge.

GLASS CUTTER

The little glass cutter is readily available in hardware stores, and a mosaicist can quickly become proficient in cutting all types of stained glass and mirror. With care, these materials can be cut using a mosaic nipper, but for long, clean and exacting cuts, the glass cutter is often to be preferred over the nipper.

OTHER CUTTING TOOLS

A wide assortment of tile cutters, both hand-held and floor-supported, are available; these can usually be bought or hired from tile specialists. The latter type is especially useful when cutting stubborn, unyielding and thick quarry and floor tiles.

For cutting metal items such as wire and mesh, pliers, tin snips and wire pincers should be used, all of which are readily available in most hardware stores. Implements such as craft knives, cutting blades and scissors for cutting paper, card and fibre netting can all be found in any art supplier's shop and also in hardware stores.

Using the glass cutter
Use the little wheel at the tip of the tool to score the upper surface of the glass in the direction of the desired cut. Then gently tap the underside of the scored line with the ball at the end of the tool, and the material will snap precisely and neatly in half.

Cutting gold in the Orsoni Workshop, Venice, Italy
This is a glass-chopping machine (Italian: *tagliatrice*). The top cutting blade is moved by a hand-operated wheel to fall exactly over a second cutting blade, fixed into the work-table.

3 Tesserae Materials

Mosaics have a long life since they are made from durable materials. Traditionally these are shell, mother-of-pearl, terracotta, stone, marble, hand-made glass and gold; to these may be added manufactured glass, china, tiles, slate and a miscellany of objects and hand-fired materials. Listed below are those most commonly associated with the art of mosaic making. The author has used the image of a bird throughout to illustrate the qualities of each material in a series of mosaic panels.

SMALTO / SMALTI

The earliest use of glass in mosaic-making is thought to have been during the first century AD, when it was used alongside stone and marble to make up any colour deficiencies, for instance

Above: Colour variation and qualities.

green and blue. This glass was almost lead free, and had a less reflective surface than glass has today. The techniques of making glass tesserae were at their most prolific during Byzantine times, and became particularly developed in the fifteenth and sixteenth centuries, when glass was made with new consistencies and colours.

Glass tesserae consist of a vitrifier of silica (sand or ground-down quartz pebbles), combined with what are called 'fluxes' of sodium or potassium carbonate. To this mix are added stabilizing elements such as magnesium or lead, and these are heated with colouring agents in a process called fusion, the timings and atmospheres of which are carefully controlled. Various secret formulae or recipes have been tried and tested over the many years of tesserae manufacture, and a number of these are jealously guarded in books or in the minds of the makers – wondrous alchemists that they are.

These formulae are concerned with attributes such as opacity, brilliance and colouring. The colouring agents are various, and consist of metallic irons, or combinations of oxides: for example manganese, iron and cobalt for black and brown; chrome for yellow and green, and selenium and cadmium for pink and red. Sometimes micro-crystals of glass are added as a fine dust to regulate the opacity and translucency of the finished product. During the fifteenth century, new amounts of lead oxide were added to the more traditional

Opposite page: A golden palette.

glass-making materials, and this resulted in the glass becoming much more brilliant and, for the mosaicist, much easier to cut. *Smalto antico* is a glass similar in effect to the less reflective glass of Byzantine times, and is made by adding sand to the molten glass; this gives a grainy surface.

After colouring and the fusion process, the glass is collected in long-handled spoons called *cassa* and poured onto shallow flat moulds of about 1cm (⅜in) in depth, to form either round plates called *pizze*, or oblong slabs. These are cooled under a slow, controlled process called 'annealing'. The material is then ready for cutting. The cut side of the disc is the side normally used in mosaic work, this being the most reflective. Smalti is frequently bought already cut into rectangular tesserae, varying in size from about 13–17mm (½–⅝in) by about 8–10mm (⁵⁄₁₆–⅜in), and 4–5mm (³⁄₁₆in) in depth; the irregularities of the hand-cut edges ensure a lively surface for the mosaic artist. Smalti is generally the mosaicist's most preferred of materials.

Smalti Filati: Glass Threads / Rods

Smalti filati is a material that was used in the eighteenth century by the Vatican mosaic workshop, in the execution of miniature mosaics. A piece of smalto is

Top: Bird mosaic palette (smalti) and *bottom*: finished Bird mosaic (smalti).

heated over a flame, and, when molten, is drawn, using tweezers, into a long thread; this is then cut into tiny pieces, quite often smaller than 1mm in diameter. It is used, cut side uppermost, for micro-mosaics.

The colours of smalti available for the mosaicist today are many – some glassmakers stock up to 5,000 colours! However, a useful working number would be between twenty and fifty. This little panel of bright colours uses about nine. The mosaic is left ungrouted for maximum colour intensity.

Traditionally smalti were ungrouted, each tessera being pressed into mortar

Right: Vatican workshop: making *smalti filati*.

up to at least three-quarters of its thickness. By using this method, the mosaic is in effect self-grouted; the cement surrounds and holds each piece securely, yet its surface stands clear of the mortar and so retains its reflective intensity.

GOLD SMALTI

Gold smalti or metal leaf glass consists of three strata. A layer of backing glass 4–7mm (³⁄₁₆–¼in) thick acts as a support; this may be coloured to enrich the density of the metal leaf which is placed on top and then covered by an upper layer of very thinly blown glass – the *cartellina* or *cristallina*. This upper layer

Above: Gold smalti – front.

Above: Gold smalti – backing glass.

Above: Gold smalti sample.

acts as a protector for the metal, and it too may be coloured to produce golds of many colours: rich yellow, blues, greens, reds and white. The gold leaf can vary in thickness, being usually around 15 micrometres, or 0.15 thousandths of a millimetre! One cubic centimetre of gold is beaten to cover 6sq m (64sq ft).

The gold smalti may be plain or rippled on the surface, and is generally sold by the kilogram. It can be bought in the form of squares known as *piastre* which measure 80 x 80mm (3 x 3in), approximately thirteen of such *piastre* making up one kilogram. Usually it is bought already cut into squares, either 20 x 20mm (¾ x ¾in), or 10 x 10mm (³⁄₈ x ³⁄₈in); 10kg (22lb) of the latter would cover about 1sq m (10.8sq ft).

Traditionally gold is placed on walls and pressed into a mortar at an angle so

as to reflect light and bounce it back to the spectator. By raising the tesserae in this way, shadows are created which produce an exciting and living surface. White gold reflects, acting more like a mirror than yellow gold, and its surface colour appears to range from brilliant white to darkest grey.

The birds in this mosaic are made primarily of coloured gold: deep and pale yellow, pink and white. The turquoise colour is obtained by reversing the tesserae so that the metal shows through the aquamarine backing glass. The curving stem of the design is of rich rippled gold standing proud of the matt ceramic background. White rippled gold is used intermittently to enliven the background area.

VITREOUS GLASS

This is a manufactured glass produced commercially for the building trade. It is made initially like smalti but is then cut into uniform shapes, most commonly 20 x 20mm (¾ x ¾in), and fixed onto gummed paper sheets or netting, 300 x 300mm (12 x 12in) in size. The sides of each tessera are bevelled, the bottom edge/surface is grooved for better adhesion into the mortar (this side is sometimes used uppermost for a textural effect), and the top edge/surface is smooth, which reduces the reflective quality of the glass.

The colour ranges are wide and various, and include primary colours, flesh tones and ordinary colours. One range has copper dust added to the glass at the time of smelting, which creates an iridescent finish. The ranges are constantly changing so it is advisable to buy sufficient of each colour at a time since subsequent orders may vary slightly in hue.

Vitreous glass is a relatively inexpensive material and can be bought by shade or as a mixed bag. The latter is particularly useful when setting out to

Above: Bird mosaic palette (vitreous glass).

Above: Bird mosaic (vitreous glass).

make mosaics with children, and when large areas need to be covered. The bevelled edge can assist when working in relief or sculpturally, as the glass can be applied to a contoured surface up to a 90° angle.

The uniformity of vitreous glass makes it an ideal material when a smooth surface is necessary, such as for a swimming pool, a floor or a table. However, this very uniformity can lead to the creation of surfaces which lack life and interest, so try to counteract this by introducing movement or curves into the design, as illustrated in the flowers and grass, or by subtle changes of colour.

Above: Bird mosaic palette (ceramic).

CERAMIC

Mosaic Ceramic Tiles

These tiles are of uniform shape, are generally straight-sided, and come in various sizes. Unglazed tiles are porous and coloured throughout, and come in a wide range of matt finishes and colour. The palette is made up of rich earth colours and is soft in tone, and includes black, white, terracotta, pink, ochres, and mottled effects.

Glazed tiles have a shiny surface on top of an unglazed tile. An easily accessible and inexpensive material, ceramic tiles are invaluable in creating a Roman-type or muted palette of colours for floors or larger areas.

The muted tones of unglazed ceramic tiles often lend themselves to designs using a limited palette. Simple images of dark on light or light on dark, with a defined linear form, create strong, memorable images, as the Romans were well aware. Use glazed tiles to create highlights in the background and to keep the surface interesting.

Ceramic Household Tiles

Household tiles provide a constant source of material in an inexhaustible

Below: Bird mosaic (ceramic).

CHINA

China includes such diverse items as cups, tureens, teapots and dishes, all having inherent qualities which can be used in mosaic, such as curved handles, lids with knobs, provocative spouts and richly decorated borders.

If using china outside, be aware that not all earthenware is frost-proof and that not all glazes can withstand the ravages of the weather. While the crazing of some glazes may add to the surface richness, the unplanned cracking and lifting of glazes may not.

By choosing and cutting carefully, the unique qualities in china of colour, glaze and texture can be put together to create mosaics of unparalleled richness, with surfaces alive with light and movement. Such a surface is at its most animated outdoors, where the shifting sunlight gives day-long movement, or indoors in a situation where it is enriched by artificial spotlighting.

Above: Bird mosaic palette (ceramic tiles).

Left: Bird mosaic (ceramic tiles).

range of finishes and colours. The tiles may be glazed, metallic, ridged, plain, dull, patterned, shaped, thin, thick: the list is endless. Create exciting effects by putting matt surfaces against shiny ones, large against small, plain against patterned. Four tiles were used to create this mosaic: one terracotta floor tile; two plain tiles, one in cream and one in blue; and one patterned tile with an image of a bird. Cut up and reassembled, a unique tile is made with the characteristics of each former tile much enriched. Antonio Gaudí used tiles in his creations in Parc Güell, often cutting up whole tiles – *azuelejos* – which were native to his homeland and reassembling them.

Above: **Elaine M. Goodwin and Group 5: Animal Farm Mosaic, Exeter, England, 1994** The wall is made of china and tiles. Teapot lids are used in the tree canopies. Yellow lids make a lemon tree.

Above: Bird mosaic palette (china).

Left: Bird mosaic palette (marble).

Below: Bird mosaic (marble).

Above: Bird mosaic (china).

MARBLE

Marble is the traditional material of Roman floor mosaics. It is a rock, composed mainly of calcium carbonate, which is crystalline in appearance and coloured by the presence of minerals in the earth. Marble can appear in many colour variations, including white from Carrara or the Middle East, pink from Verona, yellow from Sienna, as well as green, blue-grey, rose and black.

When cut, marble has a sparkling appearance, which often exposes irregularities of grain and colour: these can be exploited to full advantage by the mosaic artist. Marble can be bought already polished to a high gloss, but although this will heighten the colour considerably and give a smooth and level surface, it may also be to the detriment of its crystalline qualities.

The marble for this little bird was cut using the hammer and hardie. It is quite possible to create very small tesserae, even down to 1mm (1⁄16in), as were used in Hellenic times, although more usually tesserae are used in sizes from

5mm (³⁄₁₆in) to 20mm (¾in). The cut and unpolished surface has been used alongside polished marble to show the variations of colour and texture.

PEBBLES

Pebbles are rounded or ovoidal stones that have been smoothed by the river or the sea. They have natural colours, and can be banded or multi-toned. Generally – and historically – they are used uncut, the design of the work depending on their size and colour. It is important to store pebbles by colour coding, size, shape and unusual features.

MOTHER OF PEARL

The beautiful iridescent inner lining of the shell, usually of the pearl oyster, is used in mosaic making. It is formed in layers of conchiferous material and calcium carbonate, and can be cut – very carefully – with a bandsaw or diamond blade. In the sixth-century mosaic of the Empress Theodora in the church of San Vitale in Ravenna, in Italy, it is possible to see mother-of-pearl cut into discs to imitate precious stones for the elaborate diadem worn by the Byzantine empress.

Black and white pebble mosaics rely heavily on *chiaroscuro* – light against dark – and on the modelling of the contours – *andamento* – to separate the image from the background. This can be further helped by grading the pebbles by size and density of colour.

The mosaic was sealed after cleaning to retain the colour of the pebbles as if they were wet, but without a highly glossy or varnished finish. Mother-of-pearl is used to give an iridescent outline to the back of the bird. The shells are cut as tesserae.

Above: Bird mosaic palette (pebbles and mother-of-pearl).

Right: Bird mosaic (pebbles / mother of pearl).

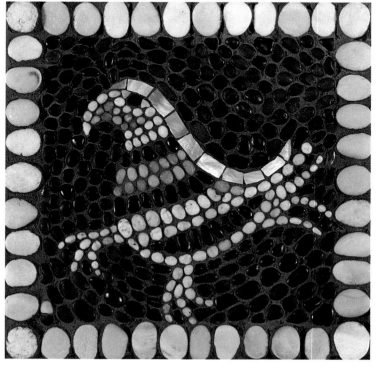

MISCELLANEOUS

Many other materials can be used in mosaic to give an interesting surface: each has its own particular quality, and for greatest effect and appeal, must be used with an understanding of its properties. Materials can be intermixed to create a variety of textures and finishes.

Slate

This consists of a clay schist of blue, green or grey colour, and is used for its soft matt sheen. Its layers can be sliced apart using a palette knife or mason's hammer and chisel, and then cut to shape as required.

Shells

These can be found in a great number of colours and sizes. They can be used either way up, and must be pressed firmly into a cement mortar to counteract any fragility.

Granite

This is used for its colour, which may be grey, white or pink, and for the characteristic sparkle of mica and feldspar that is one of its particular properties. It is cut with a hammer and chisel.

Stone

A wide variety of stone can be used in mosaic to create different effects, including porphyry, a reddish colour; chalcedony, a quartz with a grey-like finish; jasper, an opaque variegated quartz; and onyx, a transparent whitish quartz. These are cut to manageable sizes using a masonry chisel and hammer.

Semi-precious stones

Agate, a banded quartz ranging from blue to orange in colour; lapis lazuli; turquoise; and tiger eye are just some of the possible semi-precious stones that can be used to excellent effect in mosaic.

Left: Miscellaneous materials.

Glass Globules

These are manufactured glass baubles, and exist in a range of sizes and colours. Gold, silver or aluminium leaf can be stuck to the transparent bases using a PVA adhesive, which allows a glowing colour to show through.

Mirror

Mirror is used in mosaic to enliven a surface, and to give illusory effects, both indoors and outdoors. It is generally cut with a glass cutter to the required shapes. When using mirror, it is advisable to seal the back with a sealant before embedding the pieces in the mortar, in order to prevent any deterioration of the 'silvering'.

Self-Made

Mosaic tesserae and shapes can be cast, formed and glazed in a kiln. Gustav Klimt had tesserae made in clay and finished to his exact requirements. Smalti can be heated to melting point and allowed to fuse to give brilliant colour combinations.

Perishable Materials

Wood, card, paper, seeds: these are some of the materials that can be used with a temporary result. Birds' feathers were used by the Aztecs to make mosaic head-dresses in stunning colour combinations.

4 Bases

Mosaic can be fixed to a variety of bases. The choice is often determined by the positioning or siting of the mosaic, whether it is to be on a ceiling or a floor, wall-hung or free-standing, inside or outside.

PAPER

Mosaics can be constructed directly onto paper or card by people of all ages and abilities. The tesserae are also made from paper and may be of any shape or size and of mixed textures, weight and colour. Two principles of traditional mosaic making should always be observed: first, the tesserae must not overlap, one upon another; and second, they must not touch each other – a gap must be left between the paper tesserae, allowing the background colour to show through: in effect the backing card or paper becomes the grout.

Paper is also used as a temporary backing material on which to create mosaics in the reverse or indirect method. Strong brown wrapping paper is ideal, and can be bought in sheets of varying size or on a roll of varying widths.

WOOD

Wood provides an excellent base for portable mosaics, and plywood is ideal. It can be cut to any shape or size – round, square, rectangular or irregular – and should be no less than ½in (12mm) thick and no larger than about 39in (1m) in width.

Mosaics on wood should not be placed outside where damp or humid conditions could warp the base and thereby cause the mosaic to lift. If situated inside the house where there is a possibility of occasional humidity or dampness, such as in a bathroom or kitchen, it is advisable to use a marine or exterior grade plywood, in which the wood layers are bonded together with resin. All cut or exposed areas should be sealed or covered.

Wooden furniture – and this might include tables, chairs and cupboard doors – or surfaces made of wood with a recess which would take a mosaic, can all be considered functional and suitable bases for mosaic making.

TERRACOTTA

Garden centres and hardware stores stock a wide variety of terracotta pots, plaques and dishes, and these make superb ready-made bases for mosaics. Choose shapes and designs which appeal, and which will respond favourably to having a mosaic skin. Ideally select those with a lip or edge that the mosaic can be worked up to or into, because this will protect the mosaic from rain or watering.

Similarly, if pots are to be placed outside it is advisable to buy a frost-proof variety. Take great care when lifting the pot or terracotta object when it is completed, as the risk of it cracking or breaking is still high.

NET

Glass-fibre netting provides a versatile backing material for mosaic and can be cut to any size or shape; thus very large

Opposite page: **Terracotta pot**
This elegant terracotta pot has a design of golden birds on a white ceramic background. Mosaic silvered mirror glass is used to enliven the surface. The pot provides an eloquent point of focus in a garden.

Above: **Paper lizard, 122 x 244cm (8 x 4ft)**
A paper mosaic on hardboard made at Flinders University, Adelaide, Australia, with the author and students; the strong colours create a vibrant design which hints at aboriginal dot paintings.

Above: **A small decorative plaque**
Made from concrete with additional pigment, this little plaque uses mosaic of one colour in the background to offset the bird design.

mosaics can be cut to manageable sizes and pieced together at site. This means that mosaics can be made in the studio and transported on the net backing, and reassembled inside or outside. The strong fibre netting can support mosaics made of glass, ceramic and even china. It is bought in single sheets, or on a roll of approximately 100m (395ft) in length and 100cm (39in) in width.

The flexible nature of net as a backing material means that when a mosaic is completed, it can also be wrapped around cylindrical forms and both convex and concave objects, and grouted in the normal manner after fixing.

CONCRETE AND STONE

Bases made from concrete, stone or reconstituted stone provide exciting and diverse backing materials. These may be found as pillars, steps, slabs, window-sills and pre-formed shapes. Mosaic can transform or complement the neutral colours and enhance the form. Be sure that the base is sound and secure, and free from paint, grease and dust.

A final thorough cleaning using white spirit after stripping off old paint or removing traces of dirt will ensure an excellent setting base.

BRICK WALLS, PATHWAYS, GROTTOES

Potential bases with uneven surfaces such as old walls, paths and grottoes, if basically sound and secure, can be rendered first to give a more welcome, smooth surface upon which to design and create the mosaic. This is done with an initial coat of sand and cement mortar, and trowelled to a fine finish.

THREE-DIMENSIONAL (CEMENT)

Free-standing objects or sculptures can be used as a base for mosaic, but an armature of iron or wire should be used. This is worked upon to the desired shape using chicken wire, steel wire, wire netting or wire mesh. Layers of gauze or cloth soaked in a cement slurry are then used to mould the shape to a smooth form with an even cement finish. The mosaic will then adhere to this unique base.

The possible disadvantage of a three-dimensional base is its weight. Concrete, iron and mosaic when combined are inevitably exceedingly heavy, difficult to manoeuvre while being worked on, and also equally difficult to transport.

5 Adhesives

When a mosaic is made, the tesserae – which may be made of various materials – are stuck onto or pressed into a base, using an adhesive. Several different adhesives are used for this purpose, the most important ones being gum, PVA, epoxy resin and cement.

When using any adhesive, observe the highest protection procedures for health and safety reasons, since many adhesives contain ingredients that may be irritants. If it comes into contact with the skin, wash it off with copious amounts of water. Read and comply with the instructions that come with all these products.

GUM

This is a water-soluble, honey-coloured adhesive. In the direct method it can stick all paper and card tesserae to similarly made backings of card, paper and hardboard; it is applied evenly using a brush or spatula. In the more commonly used indirect method, gum is used to stick all the inverted tesserae – whether made of glass, marble, or ceramic – onto a strong paper base for a temporary hold before the sheet is transferred and turned over into a permanent position and the paper backing washed off.

Sheets of uncut mosaic squares are often presented on a gummed paper backing, and after buying, these sheets must be soaked to remove the backing before the mosaics are sorted and stored for use.

POLYVINYL ACETATE (PVA)

This adhesive is much used in mosaic making for bonding materials together, for both interior or exterior use, provided one or more of the materials is porous. It can also be used as a sealer for wood, stone, terracotta and concrete prior to making a mosaic. It is a white, viscous preparation which is colourless when it dries, and it can be applied with a brush, a spatula or a spreader. For sealing, use PVA diluted in the correct proportion of one part PVA to five parts water, and allow it to dry thoroughly before working.

For indoor use on wood and other materials, apply undiluted and fix the tesserae applying moderate pressure.

For external use, use an exterior grade PVA. The product is waterproof only when mixed with cement, usually in the ratio of one part PVA, one part water and two parts cement. However, it is not suitable for use on areas which are constantly immersed in water, such as bird baths and decorative water containers. Excess and spilt PVA should be cleaned up with a damp cloth or rinsed clean before it dries.

EPOXY RESIN

This is a two-part adhesive often found in two tubes, one containing the resin, the other the hardener. The two must be mixed well together in equal proportions, and then spread onto one or both of the surfaces which are to be

bonded; allow sufficient time for the two surfaces to become tacky before pressing them together. An immediate impact bond is formed, which should be clamped or held together until set – this will depend on the ambient temperature and how thickly the resin glue has been applied to the surfaces.

Chemical binding of this nature is extremely strong and can withstand damp and watery conditions. It is excellent for use out of doors or in humid situations.

CEMENT ADHESIVE

A number of cement-based tile adhesives are available that are excellent for use in mosaic making. They can be bought in bags from 2kg (4.5lb) up to 22kg (50lb). Do make sure that they contain Portland cement as a base, and that they are grey in colour rather than white: this will allow the colour of the mosaic materials to be as true as possible.

The adhesive must be mixed in a container with cold water to a firm consistency, and the resulting mortar applied to a dry surface using a trowel or palette knife. The tiles are then pressed firmly into position to give a good contact. In normal conditions each application has about 20 minutes of working time, so it is advisable to make up and spread only small amounts at a time. Tiles can be adjusted for up to 20–30 minutes after fixing.

A polymer additive or plasticizer can be bought and added when mixing the mortar to enhance the adhesive qualities and give more flexibility; this should be added to the water with one volume of plasticizer to two volumes of water. Add this to the cement adhesive, and mix until it reaches the required consistency. It is advisable to follow this extra procedure when making mosaics for wet conditions, to reduce water permeability. Clean off any surplus adhesive quickly with a knife or cloth before the mortar has time to set.

CEMENT

Cement is made by calcining or burning lime and clay at high temperatures of 1,500°C, and then reducing the clinker residue to a finely ground, grey powder. It is a natural binder and often goes under the name of Portland cement, so-called because its colour closely resembles Portland stone, a fine limestone used in building.

Cement is seldom used on its own in mosaic making, but is mixed with sand to give a strong mortar with excellent adhesive properties. Fine-grain sands such as Devon red, brown, silver or yellow sand can be used to give colour as well as strength to the mortar. Colour can be further distinguished by using cement pigments: these are permanent light- and heat-fast products, comprising of synthetic oxides combined with a plasticizer. The colours can be used singly, or intermixed to give a wide selection of shades; primarily they are bought in red, black, brown, blue, yellow and green. Add them cautiously at the dry stage of mixing, using approximately 10g (0.4oz) for each 10kg (22lb) of cement. It is always advisable to carry out some sample test-pieces beforehand to ascertain the degree of colour intensity.

When making up the mortar, use finely-sieved sand, and colour pigment if required, and mix with the cement. The ratio is three or four parts of sand to one part of cement. Mix it thoroughly in a plastic bowl, with protected hands, or on a flat surface with a trowel. Add the water, making a well in the mixture in

Opposite page: **Mixing cement**
Pouring water into a sand/cement mix. The 'well' helps contain the water while mixing with the trowel.

which to pour it, and using a trowel, mix to a fairly stiff consistency.

The surface to be covered or rendered may be of stone, brick or concrete. Wet the surface well and add a coat of cement slurry before the mortar is trowelled on. The slurry is made of the same mortar mix but diluted to a runny paste. This is brushed over the freshly wetted surface, and acts like a bonding adhesive between the surface and the mortar. The mortar is then trowelled smoothly onto the area, and the tesserae fixed, unit by unit. It is as well to mix up smallish quantities at a time, as the cement mortar sets quite rapidly. For larger areas such as wall murals, approximately one square metre of quite intricate mosaic work can be fixed directly at site during the course of one working day.

To retard the drying time, a mortar plasticizer can be added to the cement mortar at the mixing stage. It is easiest to add this to the water used for mixing the cement and sand together, and can greatly improve the workability and plasticity of the mix. In effect it replaces the traditional use of hydrated lime by reducing the drying time and giving a more malleable mortar. Ideally the setting time for cement should be long and slow, to allow it to cure and harden to its maximum strength. A polythene sheet can be used to cover the mosaic after a day's work to protect and aid the setting process, and to prevent cracking and crazing.

When preparing setting beds for floors and external paving mosaics, concrete should be made by mixing cement with gravel, stone or other aggregates: this increases the strength of the mixture and provides a sound under-base. Concrete can be further strengthened by reinforcing it with steel mesh or rods embedded halfway up its depth; this is useful when making concrete paving slabs or stepping stones. In sculptural or three-dimensional works, an iron armature provides an invaluable support for the structure; it can be built upon using cement mortar to mould the form.

Vinyl or latex gloves should be worn at all times when dealing with cement and plasticizers: because these substances are alkaline and therefore caustic, they can be an irritant to the skin.

Experiment with and enjoy this material. It is a cheap, versatile and exciting product, and once understood, is wonderful in adapting to the diverse methods used in creating mosaics. Given a desert island with sand, sea and shells, my luxury would naturally be bags and bags of cement – a mosaicist's heaven. Of course, in the very real everyday world, the sand and the water must be salt free....

6 Design

The designing of a mosaic involves assimilating a number of factors, and it is well worth allowing some time to muse over and consider these factors carefully before picking up the mosaic nippers and beginning work.

INSPIRATIONAL SOURCES

Make sure you always carry, or have near at hand, a sketch-pad and pencil which is small enough to use on any occasion. This can be used to draw in, and to make notes on scenes or happenings that have caught the imagination or pleased the eye, things that one can ruminate over as concepts for possible mosaic making. These initial recordings are the sound and true responses of the individual to his or her life and environment.

These sketches may be sourced from cityscapes, which abound in exciting materials – glass, steel, brick and stone – or they may come from a juxtaposition of architectural shapes and colour combinations, or from pure pictorial arrangements. Nature also yields quantities of organic forms, and decorative imagery of unsurpassable beauty with superb gradations of colour in leaf, flower and tree. Animals and birds provide strong and easily adapted forms for mosaic work, and have been used as sources of imagery in all cultures and centuries.

Deserts, mountains and the sea offer invaluable sources for design, allowing emotive mood combinations. Feelings evoked may include tranquillity, might, contemplation, terror, peace, anger – a variety of passions and responses which can be interpreted through colour combinations and direction or movement of the material. A personal religion or deeply held belief and conviction can be manifested through form and symbolism.

Books, magazines, museums and historic collections should be veritable treasure troves for ideas and inspiration. The domestic environment can yield an exciting and intimate source of imagery: a bowl of fruit or flowers, a favourite material or object. Anniversaries, occupations, logos, names and dates – in fact, anything which has a direct and unique meaning for the creator can stimulate initial ideas for a design.

Left: Drawing table, with inspirational source material.

THE DRAWING

The design must next be translated into the drawing, and this may be representational or abstract, or it may combine elements of both. Figurative or landscape images need to be translated into a usable form, and generally this is done by reducing the lines of the image into their basic and essential components; from these simplest beginnings the drawing for mosaicing is constructed.

If the image is to be symbolic, it is necessary to exaggerate or develop the most salient features or meaning. For abstract work, single out the important dynamics, colours, movements and rhythms; for lettering and logos, pinpoint the most striking elements and work from these: finally, for mosaics to be composed geometrically and with pattern, work out the placings and positionings and adapt the design accordingly. The resultant drawing is then worked upon to produce a 'cartoon' or working drawing; this often benefits from the firming up of any defining lines using a felt-tipped pen, and marking in the general direction of the flow of the tesserae. In mosaic making, this coursing of the material is called *andamento*, and may emphasize the circular, horizontal, vertical or sinuous arrangement of the tesserae.

It is important at this stage to consider the size of the image relative to its backing base, and its position on this base. Be aware of the placing of the image in its background, and whether it should touch the edge, neatly fit in it, or go beyond it. If designing a mosaic for a specific location – a wall, niche or floor – position the cartoon, which is full size, *in situ* and decide on any changes, and also ascertain how it is going to be viewed. Other considerations might include noting where the light source is, or whether the finished mosaic will be viewed mostly by day or by night, from a distance or at close quarters, and whether it is to complement or contrast with its surroundings and environment.

TRANSFERRING THE DRAWING

The cartoon or drawing must next be transferred to the base on which it is to be worked. Many cartoons can simply be traced either directly or in reverse using greaseproof or tracing paper and a graphite pencil. The tracing paper is placed over the design, which is then

Opposite page:
Eight-bird table
The imagery was drawn from nature: a circular grouping of eight birds for a summer garden table. The birds evoke characteristics of the species, not any particular type.

Far left: **Initial drawing**
Showing the major lines of movement and direction.

Left: **Abstract panel**
The finished design. Harmonious areas of rhythm and movement illustrating the aspect of *andamento* in a sample panel.

outlined in pencil. By turning the paper over, placing it on the base and then drawing over the outline which is now on the back, the reverse of the image that is on the paper will be transferred to the base. This is also a preparation for the indirect method of working, in which turning the paper over once again and re-outlining the original tracing of the image gives a copy of the initial drawing.

Another option is to place carbon paper under the image and draw over this for a direct transference. If working directly into cement, the design can be transferred by eye using a brush and a diluted permanent acrylic paint or a round-ended knife to mark the outlines. For large work, tracing paper or plastic sheeting can be put over the cartoon and the outlines drawn onto it in felt pen, or pen and inks. Turn this over and retrace the outline before laying it, front side up, onto moist cement mortar: this will give a clear imprint of the original cartoon. Alternatively the cartoon may be pricked through onto the setting cement using a prodder or sharp blade; these markings may then need to be more clearly defined by painting directly onto the surface using a brush.

Photocopying machines provide a moderately cheap way of enlarging or reducing a design to fit all requirements, and can dispense with having to utilize the system of 'squaring up': this is when the drawing is covered with a network of identical squares, and the same number of squares, but of larger dimension, is drawn up on another sheet of paper. The part of the drawing in each square is then transposed to its larger counterpart for a larger and similar version. Drawings can also be reduced in this manner.

Whatever method is used to transfer the design, it should not be thought of as something rigid, to be slavishly adhered to: rather, it must be considered as a helpful guide, something to give direction and confidence to the creator who will find, as the mosaic progresses, that it will develop its own momentum – thus sometimes it will override the initial design, and will 'take off' in directions unimagined at the outset. This spontaneity can add life and interest to the mosaic, and it should be allowed to develop within the overall spirit of the creation.

Beautifully composed templates with each tessera drawn stone by stone may be fine for producing copies, but by doing this, mosaic making may be reduced to a process of 'creating by numbers': the artist can become enslaved by a given design, and the pleasure of creating something that contains an element of the unknown is thereby greatly reduced. An overly academic or pedantic process can prevent a work of the imagination from becoming an object of desire!

Right: **A facsimile or copy of a mosaic. Mosaic class, Ravenna, Italy**

A facsimile or copy requires the cartoon to be drawn tessera by tessera. This is done by drawing in ink onto paper placed over the image or photo. The drawing is turned over, redrawn and laid onto fresh lime and laboriously copied.

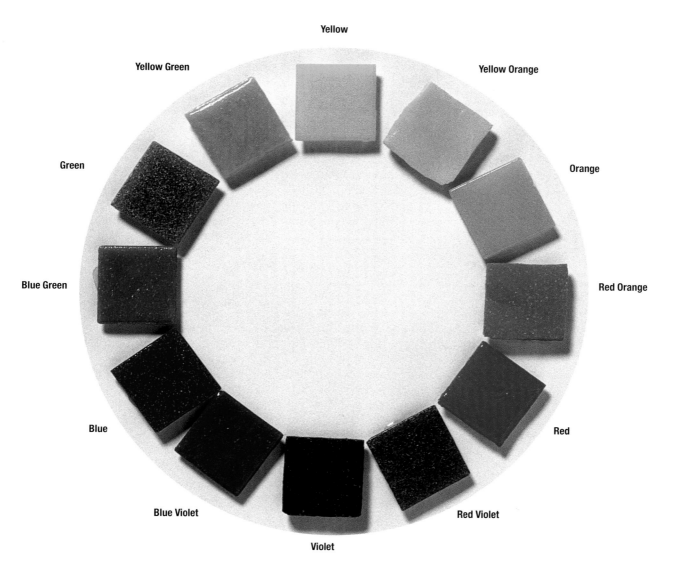

Yellow

Yellow Green · · Yellow Orange

Green · · Orange

Blue Green · · Red Orange

Blue · · Red

Blue Violet · · Red Violet

Violet

COLOUR

Colour can be one of the more immediate considerations when making a mosaic, and should be thought about carefully and with understanding, whether using a limited palette of colours or a riotous one. Black and white designs, or whites on black and blacks on white, perhaps with the inclusion of one or two colours, can produce effective and beautiful results, sometimes recalling ancient Roman mosaics or evoking strong graphic imagery.

Mosaics created with colour must be composed according to how the colours relate when juxtaposed one with another; this enables the mosaicist to achieve a diversity of effects. There are seven accepted colour components, devised by Johannes Itten at the Bauhaus in the 1920s, which can be considered when composing with colour: hue,

Above: The colour wheel.

cold/warm, light/dark, complementary, simultaneous, saturation and extension. Each to a certain degree is translated into mosaic via symbolism, emotion or the purely visual.

Colour is a strong force. It was thoroughly understood by the early Byzantine mosaicists, and to understand it from an aesthetic and artistic viewpoint today, it is imperative to have some knowledge of the colour circle, and a basic understanding of how to use it. The following section describes the colour components to consider:

Hue

These are pure, undiluted colours, the most intense being the primaries: red, blue and yellow. The secondary colours – green, orange and violet – are less strong, and the tertiary colours are even less intense.

Mosaics of great decorative quality and delight can be made by using only simple colour contrasts, and by juxtaposing one pure colour with another. This simple enjoyment can be seen in folk art, illuminated manuscripts, and the work of modern movements such as the De Stijl.

Cold/Warm

Colours can be divided into temperature sensations. Thus blue/green and red/orange on the left and right of the colour circle have the strongest cold/warm contrast, the colours on the right of the colour wheel being generally regarded as warm, and the colours on the left as cold. However, each colour is always evaluated in relation to its contrast with another: so for example red/violet is warm when contrasted to blue, but cold when contrasted to orange. Decorative interior mosaics may rely on creating particular colour combinations of colour to 'warm up' an especially cold colour scheme, or vice versa.

Light/Dark

This places the brilliance of one colour and the darkness of another in immediate contrast. The strongest expression of brilliance is black/white. In colour terms it is yellow/violet, located at the apex and bottom of the colour circle, which form the strongest light/dark colour contrast.

Lightness or brightness depends on how much white or black is mixed with the colour. This can be chosen as single ready-made units of coloured tesserae from a mosaic stockist's sample chart.

Complementary

Colours that are complementary are found diametrically opposite each other in the colour circle. Whichever pair of complementaries is chosen, all three primaries are always present: for example blue/orange (red and yellow); red/green (blue and yellow). When complementary colours are mixed together, a neutral grey colour is formed. Thus when viewed from a distance the complementary colours of mosaic look grey and their unique colour is lost, but when put adjacent to each other, each immediately incites a maximum vividness.

It is no accident that at Galla Placidia in Ravenna, in Italy, the deep blue background of the Byzantine mosaic is viewed in light that seeps through alabaster windows; these have an orange glow and give a soft grey light and provide an ambient atmosphere in which to experience the work.

Simultaneous

Each colour simultaneously generates its complementary colour to a greater or lesser degree for the viewer. However, only the eye seeks this harmony – not the camera. In mosaic this can be particularly apparent in the grout. Mosaics are often grouted with Portland cement which, by a lucky accident of fate, tends to be a neutral grey in colour; thus in a predominantly yellow mosaic, the grouting will appear violet-tinged, and the grout of a red mosaic area will appear greenish. Any two colours not diametrically opposed in the colour circle will tend towards their complementaries and set off new and dynamic colour effects.

This shifting to maintain colour stability was used for maximum effect in Byzantine times to dematerialize an image and encourage a spiritual response to a mosaic.

Saturation

This is the contrast between the purity and intensity of a colour set against a dull and diluted colour. In mosaic, when colours are unable physically to be mixed with white and black, dull tones must be placed beside vivid tones to create varying degrees of dull/vivid contrast.

Extension

Colour can be put together in areas of any size to balance and create colour prominence. Both large and small areas can be enhanced or muted by the extent to which a quantity of dull colours is placed with vivid colours.

Composing with colour in mosaic to create harmonious colour resonances therefore relies on numerous factors, the only certainty being that whatever colour is used, it is always seen in relation to its surroundings. It is a wondrously exhilarating exercise placing tesserae of one colour alongside another and experiencing the result. When composing colour palettes, take care never to shy away from experimenting – develop confidence in placing one colour against another, and be prepared to allow for change in an initially conceived idea.

OTHER POINTS OF CONSIDERATION

The mosaic materials can now be chosen with reference to specific qualities. The materials should be selected with regard to their surface texture. Unglazed ceramic and marble have a matt, light-absorbing surface, whereas glazed ceramic, mirror glass, gold and most china have varying degrees and angles of reflection. Consider juxtaposing one with another: the surfaces may be rough, smooth, grainy, rippled or curved, and you should be aware of how these attributes can be used.

The size of tesserae should be considered next. Some areas may demand large or uncut tesserae, while others will require intricate, finely cut or specifically shaped pieces. Larger compositions may well benefit by incorporating both large and small.

The height of the tesserae should also be thought about. Where a mosaic has no need to be absolutely flat, vary the height of the pieces, stand some on end or at angles, and occasionally lay areas at varying heights to each other. Keep in mind that height creates shadow, which can darken areas of colour or form grooves and ridges of dimness that can be incorporated into the design.

Many mosaics depend for their clarity and effect on forms of *chiaroscuro* (Italian: *chiaro* – light; and *scuro* – dark). The most extreme use would be black and white, but dark and light tones or shades of colour can be used to create strong dialogues of colour with interesting effects resulting from this contrasting of dark and light.

7 Techniques:
Eight step-by-step projects

The following eight designs illustrate the two main ways of mosaic making for today: the indirect and the direct techniques of laying and fixing tesserae. Each design utilizes a different base or support of two or three dimensions for either interior or exterior use.

In developing the designs, a comprehensive array of materials is explored, and a wide usage of adhesives is also demonstrated to fit the dictates of each work. The designs are explained and illustrated process by process to give greater insight into each technique, and to build up a grounding in the methods used.

How long does it take to make a mosaic? This is an impossible yet often asked question, and the answer depends on many factors, such as size, position, intricacy, technique and the mosaicist's experience. For the very simplest of mosaics a guideline might be two to three days minimum from concept to completion, including drawing, cutting, placing, grouting and framing. For more complex and ambitious designs allow two to three weeks, and for very large, intricate or three-dimensional mosaics allow two to three months.

THE INDIRECT TECHNIQUE

This method is used for creating a mosaic with a smooth and even surface, and is ideal for works of a precise or exacting nature: the tesserae, which must have at least one flat surface, are glued face down to strong brown paper with a soluble water-based adhesive.

First, the design is drawn on the brown paper; it is then inverted and fixed to a clean, flat working base with masking tape. The back-to-front nature of the drawing is especially apparent in asymmetrical and calligraphic designs. If the design is of large size the mosaic should be constructed in sections: make a plan of the design's main joining areas, indicating where it will most conveniently divide, then number each section on the back of the paper and mark it with positional directions – this will help considerably when the completed work is reassembled.

When the finished mosaic is taken to site it is placed, face down, into a cement bed and is carefully tamped flat. Once it has set, the brown paper can be washed off to reveal a smooth and previously unseen surface; this is then grouted to provide an even, durable, weather-proof mosaic.

THE DIRECT TECHNIQUE

This method is used when a moderately uniform or uneven surface is required. The technique encourages spontaneity and flexibility, since the process of laying the tesserae one by one is observed.

If a design is used at all, it is drawn directly onto the base and the tesserae are glued onto the base support for a permanent fixing position.

Opposite page: Fountain and three golden birds.

Above: Pedestal base – made of reconstituted stone, an ideal material on which to construct a mosaic.

DESIGN ONE: OUTDOOR GAMES TABLE

The pedestal base, bought at a garden centre, was of ideal height and dimensions for conversion to a garden games table. It was of reconstituted stone and made up of three components: a base, a central column and a corniced top.

EQUIPMENT

- Protective clothing
- Pedestal base: height 43cm (17in); top 33 x 33cm (13 x 13in). Inserts 15 x 18cm (6 x 7in)
- Gum arabic
- Mosaic nippers
- Right-angle ruler
- Pencils
- Brown paper
- Masking tape
- Brushes
- Wooden board for use as a weight and for tamping
- Trowel
- Art knife
- Notched grout spreader
- Hammer
- Felt-tipped pen
- Scissors
- Cloths
- Water container
- Cement adhesive
- Mortar plasticizer
- Cement
- Yellow sand
- Mortar cleaner

MATERIALS
Black, white and neutral unglazed ceramic mosaic tiles.

TECHNIQUE: INDIRECT, ONTO PAPER

Stage 1. The dimensions of the square top of the pedestal were drawn onto brown paper. This was secured to a work-top using masking tape. Large, uncut tesserae were fixed around the inner edge of the square using a little gum arabic applied to the front of the tile before fixing.

Stage 2. An outer border frame was built up using quarter tesserae. The border was made wide enough for any unused games pieces or counters to be placed upon it. At the end of each session of work, a wooden board was placed over the mosaic and weighted down, so as to be assured of a completely flat surface during the drying process.

The chequered board was completed using uncut and alternating black and white tesserae. Wide grouting lines were left between each tessera.

Stage 3. When dry, the mosaic was cut close to its edge clear of the brown paper, using an art knife.

Stage 4. A quantity of cement adhesive was mixed up with mortar and a cement plasticizer to make a mixture of a pliable consistency. This was trowelled onto the surface of the base, and finished with a smooth surface 2–3mm (⅛in) thick.

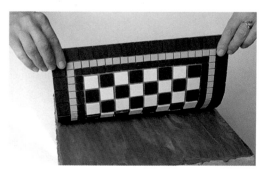

Stage 5. The finished mosaic on its paper backing was carefully positioned over the cement bed and laid in position. This is an exacting process and allows for no adjusting!

Stage 6. A piece of wood was placed on top and gently tamped down, using a hammer, to give a level surface. The cement adhesive should not rise more than half way up between the tesserae. The mosaic was then left for two to three hours to set.

Stage 7. Once assured that the mosaic was set, the paper backing was thoroughly soaked using a damp cloth, and the paper peeled away to expose the mosaic surface for the first time. Any tesserae not in line could at this stage be repositioned using a small amount of fresh cement adhesive.

Stage 8. A grout consisting of three parts yellow sand and one of cement was rubbed into the interstices or gaps left

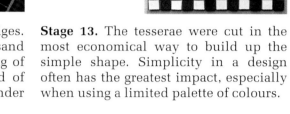

between the tesserae and at the edges. The soft yellow nature of the sand complemented the mellow colouring of the stone. The surface was cleaned of any excess grout and left to cure under damp cloths before cleaning.

Four further panels were made, drawn to represent games pieces: draughts, halma and chess.

Stage 13. The tesserae were cut in the most economical way to build up the simple shape. Simplicity in a design often has the greatest impact, especially when using a limited palette of colours.

Stage 14. The background tesserae were cut into quarters in a simple *opus tessellatum* to echo the chequerboard effect of the top.

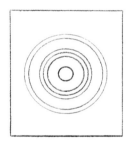

Stage 9: Draught piece (i).

Stage 10: Chess piece (knight) (ii).

Stage 11: Halma piece (iii).

Far right: The elegant games table provides a unique and all-year-round attraction for the garden or terrace. The pleasing simplicity of its form imparts a classical and timeless feel to the table, on which chess and draughts will be played. In time it will age attractively, as the reconstituted stone attracts lichen and weathering.

Stage 12. A design was drawn up on brown paper and secured to the work-top in a similar way. A single chequered border was used for the frame.

DESIGN TWO: TREE

Many mosaics are made using wood as a support. In this mosaic the wood is cut to resemble the shape of a tree. The tesserae are cut and placed to give a fairly even surface of mosaic. The gold is fixed in the 'Byzantine' manner by being positioned in the cement at an angle; this method helps to animate the otherwise flat surface.

EQUIPMENT

- Protective clothing
- Marine plywood (12mm (½in) thick), cut into a tree form 94cm (37in) high, 39cm (15½in) wide
- Saw (electric bandsaw)
- 4B pencil
- Black felt-tipped pen
- Sandpaper
- Spatula
- PVA adhesive
- Mosaic nippers
- Ready-mixed cement grout
- Cement pigment: moss green
- Cloths
- Cement adhesive
- Small palette knife
- Water containers
- Mortar cleaner
- Proprietary impact adhesive (optional)

MATERIALS

- Assorted green vitreous glass including copper vein glass
- Assorted brown vitreous glass including bronze vein glass
- Black and white vitreous glass
- Rippled and plain gold metal leaf

TECHNIQUE: DIRECT, ONTO WOOD

Stage 1. The design was drawn directly onto the wood using the pencil, then given a clearer definition using a felt-tipped pen. The outer line was cut into a tree shape using a saw, and then smoothed with sandpaper. The front, back and  edges were sealed by brushing on undiluted PVA adhesive and allowing it to dry, then a second coat was applied. The mosaic was designed for an outside, but covered terrace.

Stage 2. A small quantity of cement adhesive was made up with a little water and applied to the centre of each floral rosette. Plain gold tesserae were cut into quarters and pressed into the thickish mix, at an angle. The area was surrounded with a square of light lime-green copper glass before being shaped into random-sized circles.

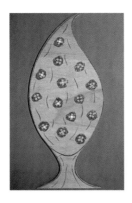 

Below: **Tree**
The tree adorns a wall on a decorative wrought-iron terrace. The restrained yet rich coloration of the mosaic gives an enchanting focal point to an arrangement of garden flower-pots.

Stage 3. All fourteen rosettes were worked on first. Each central gold tessera was placed at a different angle.

Stage 4. A rich border of green glass made up a framing canopy for the tree. Copper green glass was used to introduce small lines of iridescent colour to the design.

Stage 5. White glass, cut into quarters, was used for the inner background, following strong vertical lines in the centre of the design.

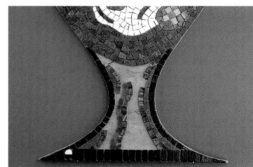

Stage 6. The trunk of the tree was built up with lines of brown, bronze-brown and black, and finally filled with rippled gold. When completed, the mosaic was edged with whole black and green tesserae to protect the edges, then it was grouted with added green cement pigment, and cleaned. The tree was fixed flush to the wall using a proprietary impact adhesive; alternatively it could have been hung using mirror plates or wire and staples. It was placed in a location where it would catch and reflect the sunlight.

DESIGN THREE: THREE GOLDEN BIRDS

The three little flying birds were designed to embellish a narrow, jutting pilaster in a garden courtyard. To minimize the depth of the mosaics and to allow for a permanent and secure all-weather placing, the birds were made on a fine-weaved netting and fixed on site. Plain and rippled gold-leaf smalti was used throughout, but mirror and gold-glazed tile or china could be substituted.

EQUIPMENT

- Protective clothing
- White drawing paper
- Soft pencils
- Black felt-tipped pen
- Mosaic nippers
- Exterior quality PVA adhesive
- Sheet of plastic or polythene 33cm (12in) square
- Fibre netting 33cm (12in) square
- Knife
- Scissors
- Ready-mixed cement grout
- Two-component epoxy resin adhesive
- Spatula
- Mortar cleaner
- Brushes
- Cloths
- Water containers

MATERIALS

- An assortment of gold-leaf smalti was used, plain and rippled. Gold or metal-backed glass could be substituted and gold-glazed chinaware or tiles.

TECHNIQUE: DIRECT, ONTO FIBRE NETTING

Stage 1: Bird drawing (i). **Stage 2:** Bird drawing (ii). **Stage 3:** Bird drawing (iii).

Three small birds measuring between 23cm (9in) and 36cm (13in) in length were drawn onto white paper and clearly outlined with a felt-tipped pen.

Stage 4. Each drawing was placed on the work-table and covered with a sheet of plastic. A piece of fibre netting of similar measurement was placed over this, with the drawing showing through. The gold tesserae were cut in half, and then into three, and shaped to form part of the wings. Each tessera was glued to the netting using PVA adhesive. The plastic sheet prevented the glue from sticking to the paper.

Stage 5. The wings were made more elaborate by using rippled and plain gold, and by inverting some of the gold to let the golden-yellow backing glass shine through. A quarter piece of gold tessera was cut into a round shape for the eye, first by cutting off the four corners diagonally and then by 'nibbling' around the edges until it reached the required size.

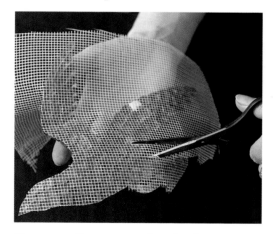

Stage 6. Once completed, the mosaic was left overnight to dry; it was then inverted and the plastic backing peeled off. It was left for a further twenty-four hours to dry thoroughly, during which time it became somewhat stiff in character. Then it was held upside-down in one hand, and cut close to the edges using the scissors.

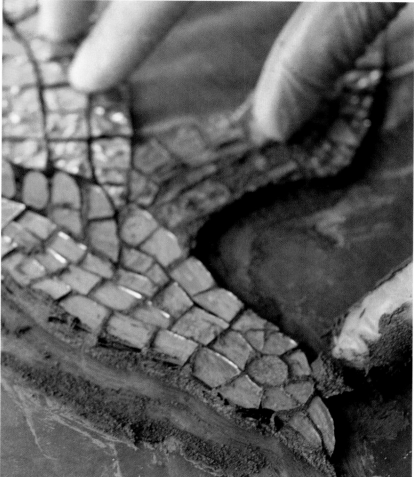

Stage 7. The shaped mosaic on its net backing was replaced on the plastic sheet, mosaic face up, and grouted using a stiff cement, sand and water mortar. Great care was taken at the edges where small tesserae were vulnerably positioned. The little bird was left to cure, and then cleaned. A sharp knife was used to release the mosaic cleanly from the protective plastic backing.

An epoxy resin was made up and spread over the back of the bird on its net; within ten minutes or so the bird could be placed into its permanent position on the pilaster. The other two birds were similarly positioned.

Opposite page:
Three golden birds
The three birds are grouped to form a delightful backdrop to the courtyard pilaster and wall. The gold glints and glimmers in the sunlight, taking full advantage of the reflective qualities of the metal leaf glass; even in winter mists the three birds shimmer in their arrested golden flight.

DESIGN FOUR: FISH DISH

A very large terracotta dish with a silicon finish and frost-proof guarantee was bought at a garden centre. The idea was to make a richly exotic centrepiece which could be both functional and decorative. By using an epoxy resin adhesive for a water-resistant fixing, it became possible for the dish to contain an inspired fish recipe for a wondrous party occasion, or simply to be placed on a table or floor to enrich a setting.

EQUIPMENT

- Protective clothing
- Terracotta dish 55cm (21½in) in diameter
- Rubber
- Pencil
- Felt-tipped pen
- Palette knife
- Epoxy resin adhesive
- Mosaic nippers
- Tweezers
- Prodders
- Glass cutter
- PVA adhesive
- Ready-mixed cement grout
- Cement pigment: black
- Cloths
- Water containers

MATERIALS

- Assorted turquoise-blue vitreous glass, including copper vein
- Copper vitreous glass
- White vitreous glass
- Matt white ceramic
- Silver smalti / sheets of silver, platinum, aluminium leaf and turquoise-blue stained glass

TECHNIQUE: DIRECT ONTO TERRACOTTA

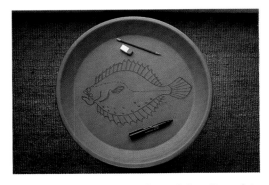

Stage 1. A large flat fish (in this instance a flounder) was drawn on the inner base of the dish and then clearly delineated in felt-tipped pen. The image was single and large, and empathetic to the circular shape of the dish.

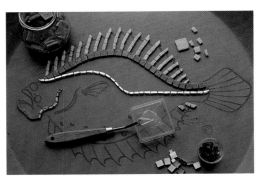

Stage 2. The central spine of the fish was defined with a single running line of silver-coloured tesserae – each tessera was cut in half and then into four, and the pieces placed end to end. Small amounts of epoxy adhesive were mixed at a time and applied to the back of each tessera before it was placed in position. The dorsal fin and jaw were outlined in different shades of blue.

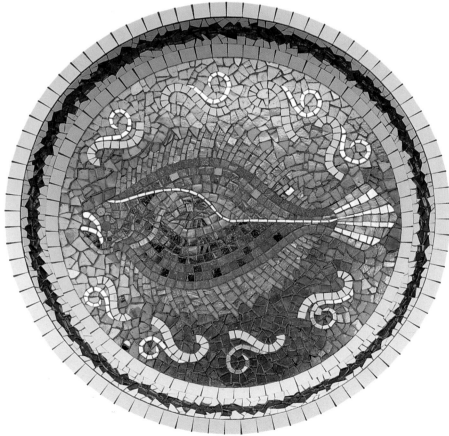

Stage 3. Both the dorsal and the ventral fin were filled in with copper-veined glass, and the back of the fish was also filled, including three inverted silver leaf tesserae. The eyes were cut, and the mouth and tail defined.

Stage 4. The fish was completed using various shades of turquoise-blue glass. Ceramic tesserae were cut to form loosely contrived wave forms. Whole ceramic tesserae were fixed around the outer and inner rim of the dish, and were made to overlap at the top inner lip.

Stage 5. The background used reverse silver smalti alongside silver-leaf-backed stained glass, in a crazed paving design: *opus palladianum*. Translucent glass, or stained glass coloured with metal oxides to give lustrous colours, was used to great advantage in this mosaic. The glass was cut with the glass cutter and nipper into random shapes, and placed on metal leaves of silver (aluminium or platinum can also be used) to display its brilliant colour. This is a much less expensive way of achieving a glowing effect when silver smalti is unavailable.

Above: The dish is of dazzling colour, richly enhancing the shallow terracotta garden dish. Placed in the right light, including candlelight, the fish appears to be swimming in a luminous and watery medium of turquoise light.

The golds of the sundial are rich, warm and sparkling – a fitting homage to the sun, the foreteller of time.

DESIGN FIVE: MILLENNIUM SUNDIAL

The sundial was made to mark the new millennium, a sun clock being an apt design with which to celebrate and announce it, and to acknowledge the previous thousand years.

The support was made of concrete, an excellent base for an outside mosaic. The gnomon or rod which indicates the time was securely fixed to the centre of the sundial's face, its position predetermining the spacing of the marks that indicated the hours. Roman numerals were used to designate the hours, thus creating a link with an earlier millennium. China and tiles were used to create a lively surface, rich in colour and texture.

EQUIPMENT

- Outdoor sundial: a circular base, a pillar, and a sundial dish 51cm (20in) in width, and height in total 92cm (36in)
- Protective clothing
- Mosaic nippers
- Soft pencils
- Compass and extension
- 360° protractor
- Exterior PVA
- Spatula
- Tweezers

- Dental probes
- Rounded and pointed palette knives
- Ready-mixed cement grout
- Cloths
- Water containers

MATERIALS

- Assorted red tiles and china
- Assorted gold tiles and china
- Assorted white glazed ceramic household tiles
- White vitreous glass
- Red vitreous glass
- Gold smalti, white and rippled

TECHNIQUE: DIRECT ONTO CONCRETE

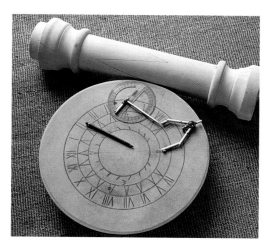

Stage 1. The hourly sun times were marked out on the face of the dial, first noting the direction of north in order to mark the position of the gnomon correctly. The radiating sunlight was drawn as decorative triangles. The shaft of the pillar had a simple, pointed, triangular design to signify the imminent millennium, with an apex to mark an end and, equally, a beginning.

Stage 2. The pillar was sealed, a small area at a time, with undiluted PVA adhesive, and the china and tile tesserae

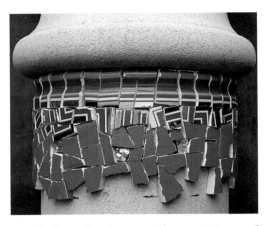

Stage 4. Simple, white household tiles were cut and placed in the remaining triangular shape. Each time another small area was sealed with a layer of PVA before the tesserae were applied.

applied to the base with a mixture of PVA, cement and water while the adhesive was still tacky. Marks were put in pencil to give an indication of the colour limit of each section of material.

Stage 5. The gnomon was securely fixed into position and the clock dial defined in tesserae of gold. The pieces were cut as accurately as possible for a clear shadow reading.

Stage 3. The red area was completely filled in for the top part of the pillar, introducing gold and other pin-points of highly reflective material.

Stage 6. Gold tesserae also provided a warm, golden sun-centre. White ceramic and vitreous glass was used in the outer surrounding bands.

Stage 7. After sealing as before, a slightly thicker mixture was made of external PVA, cement and water, and the tesserae were pressed in piece by piece.

Stage 8. The letters MM were decoratively applied to denote the year 2000, and tiles with a glazed edge were used as the outer rim. The remaining space was filled in.

Two simple, circular friezes of white ceramic and gold were placed

at the top and lower parts of the pillar. The base and underside of the dish were left undecorated, the colour and texture of the concrete being an integral aspect of the design and part of its overall visual appeal. Finally, the finished design was grouted and cleaned.

DESIGN SIX: HANGING BASKET

A mosaic hanging basket introduces the idea of working over a wire frame or armature. In this case it was pre-formed, but the same technique would be applied to any construction built up using wire or wire mesh. Among the medley of richly patterned and decorated china for the basket were some 'found' fragments dug up by chance in an English garden: a common occurrence, such china fragments probably dating from the mid-nineteenth century onwards.

EQUIPMENT

- Protective clothing
- Wire hanging basket and chain (height 68cm (27in); diameter 33cm (12in))
- Mosaic nippers
- Glass cutter
- Scrim / gauze
- Water containers
- Lidded cement containers
- Cloths
- Brushes
- Felt-tipped pen
- Small plastic rods
- Protective plastic sheeting
- Exterior PVA
- Knife

- Small trowels
- Palette knife
- Prodders
- Cement adhesive
- Ready-mixed cement grout
- Mortar cleaner

MATERIALS

- Dark blue edging tiles
- Assorted decorated blue, lilac, turquoise china and lustreware
- 'Found' garden china fragments: blue and white
- Metal leaf silver-/gold-backed opaque glass

TECHNIQUE: CEMENT ONTO A WIRE ARMATURE

Stage 1. The wire hanging basket (devoid of any plastic coating) was turned upside down so as to work on the outside. A container of slurry was made – a mixture of cement adhesive and water. Strips of gauze were thoroughly soaked, then immersed in the slurry and draped over the outside of the wire frame; this was then left to set overnight. The following day the basket was turned right side up and the inside was treated in the same manner.

Stage 2. Six plastic prodders were used to puncture the base, thereby creating water drainage holes. The gauze was then covered with a number of layers of slurry, brushed on layer by layer, to form

Opposite page: The highly decorative, hanging garden ornament is rich with colour and texture. Bright blue-and-white summer flowers are planted to create a haze of complementary colour.

a smooth cement surface. Care was taken around the chain fixtures. This was again left overnight to set.

Stage 5. A round-ended knife was ideal for defining linear movement in the mortar; then the glass was cut into long rectangular lines and applied end to end.

Stage 3. The design – a decorative arabesque of leaves, gently curving tendrils and wavy bands – was drawn onto the cement using first pencil and then felt-tipped pen.

Stage 6. The rich border colours included the 'found' garden china fragments, and tesserae of ornate design and lustrous colour.

Stage 4. A thick mixture of exterior PVA, cement adhesive and water was carefully trowelled onto the design, one small area at a time, and a radiating base design was built up, encircling the drainage rods and introducing lustreware for highlights.

Stage 7. Edging tiles were cut into strips about 2.5cm (1in) wide. The concave, unglazed backs of the tiles were filled with cement mix and pressed onto the outer rim of the basket to give a neat line of curved tiles, which both edged the basket and protected the rim. When dry, the basket was carefully grouted and cleaned; special care was taken where the chain was joined to the mosaic.

DESIGN SEVEN: GOOSE

The image of a goose was frequently portrayed during Roman times in mosaics showing Nilotic imagery. These often detailed works were found in the Roman provinces encircling the Mediterranean Sea. The bird has a good outline shape, and one particularly endearing quality – the possibility of it laying a golden egg!

The goose was purchased at a garden centre as a free-standing ornament made of reinforced concrete.

EQUIPMENT

- Protective clothing
- Three-dimensional goose (height 64cm (25in); width 54cm (21in))
- Mosaic nippers
- Charcoal pencil
- Colourless fixative
- Tweezers
- Dental probes
- File / glass paper
- Cushion / pillow
- Plastic sheeting
- Assortment of palette knives
- Cement
- Cement adhesive
- Exterior-quality PVA
- Mortar plasticizer
- Lidded cement containers
- Water containers
- Ready-mixed cement grout
- Cement pigment, black
- Cloths
- Assortment of brushes
- Mortar cleaner

MATERIALS

- Assortment of black vitreous glass, including copper vein
- Assortment of white vitreous glass including copper vein
- Copper vitreous glass
- Bronze vitreous glass
- White ceramic
- Silver smalti rippled / plain
- Gold smalti rippled / plain
- Ceramic eyes - cut from figurative china

TECHNIQUE: DIRECT, INTO CEMENT ON CONCRETE

Stage 1. Before applying the mosaic, the goose was scrubbed with water and rendered with a slurry of cement adhesive and water, using a brush and palette knife. The contours of the goose were improved to give it a good shape on which to work. A charcoal pencil was used to delineate the form and mark out separate sections for the mosaic.

Stage 2. At this stage it was easier to work on the bird on the floor – this was covered in protective plastic sheeting. After the main contours of the goose had

Stage 3. An adhesive was made of cement mixed with equal parts of PVA and plasticizer – no water – to a thick, malleable texture; this was applied in small amounts at a time, and the excess cleaned off after each mosaic application. Vitreous glass was used for the bird's body; for the feet the glass was inverted so as to show the textural side. The eyes were cut from figurative china and surrounded with rippled silver and black glass. The beak was made of gold. At some curved areas it was necessary to cut the backing glass of the gold with the nippers to form a bevel, which was filed smooth before applying.

Stage 4. The head and body were built up using vitreous glass in quarter tesserae of larger and smaller size.

Far left: The goose, its body encrusted with ornate glass and gold, stands bathed in shimmering light by a still pond.

been marked with charcoal pencil, it was sprayed with fixative; this held the drawing secure, but still allowed for any changes or adjustments.

Stage 5. Much of the mosaic making was done with the goose laid on a pillow protected with plastic sheeting. This made it easier to manoeuvre, and therefore it was easier to apply the tesserae – although care had to be taken since the goose was heavy and becoming increasingly so....

Stage 6. Gold was applied to the back, thereby creating another metallic surface so as to maximize light reflection; this is particularly effective should the goose be placed out of doors.

Stage 7. The pattern of the wings was drawn in more detail: such small areas of detailing give a pleasing overall balance when combined with larger, more straightforward sections.

Stage 8. The base was made up of silver and black tesserae. Silver is a wondrous reflector of light and movement, a factor which became more apparent when the bird was positioned outside. The completed bird was grouted with care, with a little black cement pigment added to the mix, and finally cleaned.

DESIGN EIGHT: FOUNTAIN

Certain important factors must be considered when constructing a mosaic fountain. First, the area needs to be supplied with electricity for the pump and any subsequent lighting; this is a task for a professional. The supply should be carried in heavy-duty cable so as to protect it from wear and tear and the weather. Second, the setting bed must be built up to form a sound, hard-wearing base on which to create the mosaic and contain the fountain. The position of the fountain should be in natural sunlight if possible, for maximum play of light. At night, artificial lighting can be used to create sparkling light effects.

A range of small pumps and supports can be found at garden centres and hardware stores. The size of the mosaic surround will be determined by the size and spread of the pump and the fountain water-head.

EQUIPMENT

- ◆ Protective clothing
- ◆ Fountain pump
- ◆ Pump support: diameter 66cm (26in); depth 23cm (9in)
- ◆ White marble chippings / pebbles
- ◆ Rubble / bricks / stones
- ◆ Sand, and sand with added aggregate (builders' sand)
- ◆ Cement
- ◆ Cement adhesive
- ◆ Trowels
- ◆ Length of wood 76cm (30in)
- ◆ Water containers
- ◆ Cement containers
- ◆ Mixing board
- ◆ Palette knives
- ◆ Mosaic nippers
- ◆ Glass cutter
- ◆ Knife
- ◆ Mortar cleaner / hydrochloric acid
- ◆ Brushes
- ◆ Sieve
- ◆ Masonry brush

MATERIALS

- ◆ Silver / copper mirror 3-4mm (⅛-¼in) thick
- ◆ White ceramic tiles
- ◆ Glazed white household tiles
- ◆ White china
- ◆ Rippled silver smalti
- ◆ Can of silver spray paint

TECHNIQUE: DIRECT, INTO SAND AND CEMENT MORTAR

The setting bed
A Tesserae in a setting bed
B *Nucleus*
C *Rudus*
D *Statumen*
E The ground

Above: Stages in the construction of a foundation on which to create a mosaic.

The construction of the setting bed is of paramount importance in pavimental and floor mosaic work. The foundations need to be of loose stone, brick and rubble: this is traditionally called the *statumen*, and is pressed or pounded down to provide good drainage and a firm base. The next layer, the *rudus*, is of smaller stones and rubble, and this is mixed with a layer of cement and sand with added aggregate to form an intermediary foundation layer of up to 23cm (9in). The penultimate layer, up to 10cm (4in) thick, uses a strong mortar of sand with fine aggregate and cement (and lime), and is trowelled to a smooth finish: the *nucleus*. This bed provides an excellent surface on which to add a fine layer of fixing mortar to hold the tesserae. Each layer is left to cure for a number of days in a damp – not wet – condition before applying a slurry and adding the succeeding layers of mortar.

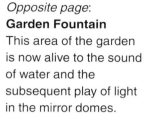

Opposite page:
Garden Fountain
This area of the garden is now alive to the sound of water and the subsequent play of light in the mirror domes.

Stage 2. A layer of fine mortar was mixed and put on top of the rudus, and levelled with the narrow strip of wood – this was drawn across the surface to ensure a smooth, even finish. The central area was tidied and finished to receive the support.

Stage 1. A foundation was made of large stones and rubble (the *statumen*); the brick surround was then cemented onto this to form a containing semi-circular shape. Next the electricity supply was laid, brought underground in heavy-duty cable to emerge in the centre of the design; the exposed wires were further protected by a piece of plastic pipe. A lower inner circle of bricks was made to fit the fountain's diameter; this was surrounded with coarse rubble, which was then covered with a sand-and-cement mortar mix (the *rudus*).

Stage 3. The support was tested for fit and then removed, so that work could continue – seated on site with legs and feet in the hole! No design was drawn, but an initial concept was developed on the theme of water and reflection while the mosaic was in process. Small mounds made of stiff cement adhesive were formed at intervals, and copper mirror tesserae were then pressed into each at various angles.

Stage 5. It was felt that more domes of smaller sizes with radiating surrounds would emphasize the watery nature of the design of the mosaic. Silver mirror of thicker quality was used for these.

Stage 4. The support was sprayed with silver, and the pump attached to the cable (after carefully reading the instructions). The mirror domes were surrounded with glazed ceramic tiles and china, pressed into a sand-and-cement mortar; for each application the surface was wetted, and a slurry applied before the mortar was trowelled onto the surface. At the end of each day's work the area was thoroughly cleaned of excess mortar, cutting close to the mosaic using a knife.

Stage 6. The remaining area was filled in with white china and occasional tesserae of rippled silver smalti; each application involved wetting the surface and brushing on the slurry, then applying a mortar made of finely sieved sand and cement. The mosaic was grouted with sieved sand, cement and black pigment, then cleaned with hydrochloric acid and water. When dry, the mosaic was brushed down with a masonry brush, to bring up the shine on the mirror and china. The support was filled with water, and the pump submerged and placed in an upright position; the cover of the support was put in place, and a layer of marble chippings spread over the whole. The electricity was then switched on!

8 Laying Mosaics:
The *Opus* Techniques

Opus / opera (pl) is Latin for 'work': in mosaic terms it is applied to the various ways of working, and describes how the tesserae are positioned and fixed in order to create particular patterning and finishes. The following pavings are traditional, and can be seen as the forerunners of mosaic paving:

Opus segmentatum: a paving of stone or marble chips within a mortar.

Opus signinum: a simple paving of mixed stone fragments or red clay pottery, sometimes very fine and often pinkish/red. The term comes from Segni in Lazio, Italy, which is famed for its red clay.

Opus alexandrinum: a paving made up of small pieces of stone, often red or purplish-red in colour (porphyry) and green (serpentine).

Opus scutulatum: a paving made up of geometric shapes, often lozenge- or diamond-shaped which comes in three different colours, forming 3D cubes or a lozenge pattern.

Opus sectile: pieces of marble and stone of specific shape – triangle, rectangle, etc. – forming a mosaic inlay of uniform design. The pieces may be two-tone or highly coloured. The technique originates in the Middle East.

Some *opus / opera* employed historically can be used today: they may be developed to convey special effects of movement or stability, or to help integrate image and ground, or to create rich textural interest. The author has made a still-life mosaic using the image of a jug (or jugs) to demonstrate each particular *opus*.

OPUS TESSELLATUM

Opus tessellatum describes a mosaic of stone or glass using tesserae of fairly uniform size and with a regular square shape. In this technique the image is surrounded by one or two lines of

Still life with two lemons
The images of the jug, dish and lemons have been outlined with one row of ceramic tesserae; this technique holds the image securely on its ground, giving an even balance between drawing and infill.

Still life with two vessels
In this mosaic deliberate use was made of *opus tessellatum* to create a background of horizontal lines of differing size and materials (smalti, glass and marble), but similar colour. In this case the images were not outlined with one line of tesserae but were left, the linear background continuing up to and beyond the image. This displayed to full effect the narrow, vertical nature of the work.

tesserae to delineate its form, and only then is the background filled in with uniform horizontal or vertical lines of tesserae. Many Roman mosaics employed this method: good examples come from Pompeii, especially the threshold mosaics depicting guard dogs – the so-called *cave canem* mosaics.

OPUS VERMICULATUM

The tesserae used in this technique are more refined in size and placing. They follow the form closely, or provide contouring detail around part of a form, their shape resembling little worms or *vermi*, from which the technique gets its name. The lines need not be made up of squared tesserae, but may be irregularly shaped and quite small.

Greek vase / Oenochoe with vine
The image of the vase is surrounded by lines of tesserae which follow the graceful curves of the vessel, exaggerating and emphasizing its form. The lines use alternating glass and ceramic tesserae. Internally, small lines of tiny irregular tesserae define and shape areas of leaf and grape in the manner of a Greco/Roman *emblema*, or insert panel.

OPUS REGULATUM / RETICULATUM

Jug and snail
In this little black and white mosaic, the grid-like network of gaps between the tesserae is grouted with an added terracotta red pigment to clearly define the grid formation.

This technique uses a grid-like effect which is formed not by the image but by the spaces between the tesserae. These are uniform and of equal size, and might be compared with a computer mosaic. The result is a work in which image and background have identical weight and identity; contours, linear markings and direction within the image or design are ignored, and the strong network of the interstices or gaps supersedes all.

The curved jug and spiralling snail shell challenge the ruthless squared network. The technique is excellent for logos and calligraphic mosaics, as any background is thoroughly integrated with the imagery.

Opposite page: **Golden vase with three birds (fire screen)**
In this mosaic two *opera* are used in conjunction with each other to emphasize two different aspects of the design. To accentuate the curving lines of the tulip forms, the background has used *opus vermiculatum* to give movement and rhythm to the long-stemmed floral image, the inspiration for which came from tiles in Istanbul in Turkey. The lower part of the mosaic uses *opus tessellatum*, as lines of tesserae are employed horizontally to stabilize the image of the vase and firmly ground it, giving weight to the lower part of the mosaic where it is fixed to the floor.

OPUS MUSIVUM

This term is thought to mean a wall or niche of a decorated *nymphaea / musaea* mosaic, one which would use any variety of mosaic materials. A more generally accepted meaning is of an all-over floor covering in mosaic. Any central insert or *emblema* is integrated within the design as a whole so there is no distinction between the centrepiece and the rest of the mosaic area.

OPUS PALLADIANUM

This is not a classical term, and may be equated to a technique similar to crazy paving. Randomly shaped pieces are tessellated together to give a background of complex yet even design; also the tesserae may be of various materials, and of varied size and shape. This is an excellent technique for filling in irregular or asymmetrical areas, whether within an image or for a background.

Mosaic pavement, Maaleh Adomim, Israel (detail)
Bunches of grapes in spreading decorative volutes, emanating from a vase, form a wonderfully spreading image as part of a floor.

Water jug and glass (detail)
When the forms are not to be delineated or given any particular prominence, *opus palladianum* is an excellent technique for giving a textured or variegated surface, as tesserae of any material or colour may be added to a greater or lesser degree.

SHELL-LIKE/SCALLOP BACKGROUND

This is not a true *opus,* but rather, is a way of laying mosaic backgrounds which has been practised from Roman times. Particularly good examples occur in Istanbul at the Great Palace, dating from the sixth century. In this technique, fan-like motifs are laid in a fairly regular way in a background, to add interest to an area which has no other images or incident.

Above: **'How to build a scalloped shell background' by Bob Field**
The drawing shows how to build up a background using tesserae to give a scalloped shell formation.

Left: **Ornamental amphora**
This elegant little amphora with its stopper would hold perfumed oil; the mosaic is for a bathroom. The scallop shell background seemed appropriate, given the connection with water and bathing, and the gentle curves it introduced added to the overall background interest.

9 Finishing and Positioning

GROUTING

Grouting is the procedure whereby all the spaces between the mosaic tesserae are filled with cement, and the mosaic gains its true identity: a unified surface made up of singular components. Grouting serves a number of purposes, the main one being that, quite apart from gaining a characteristic look, the mosaic is strengthened and made almost indestructible; its surface also becomes resistant to water and weather.

To grout or not to grout... Many Byzantine mosaics and those made in the Byzantine tradition, as in St Paul's Cathedral in London, use Italian smalti which is pressed on site into a setting bed. They are not grouted, the thick setting bed providing a secure hold which in turn partially grouts the tesserae. Smalti, with its many imperfections such as bubbles, holes and irregular surface, tends to lose some of its brilliance if grouted. Conversely, mosaics made of marble, ceramic, pebbles and manufactured glass are enhanced by grouting, the cement in the spaces or interstices adding an integral new element to the mosaic.

To maximize the effect of grouting for durability, strength and colour, it is desirable to use a cement-based grout of a grey colour. Pigments may then be added to this to complement the colours used in the mosaic.

Pigments are available in all the earth colours, including green, ochre, red, blue and black. They should be added to the cement adhesive in the ratio of 1:20. White cement can be bought to which artist's pigment can be added for brighter coloration and when integral to the design.

Add water to the cement adhesive in a plastic container or bowl, and mix with a trowel to a thick, smooth consistency. Wear gloves to work the mixture into the mosaic, taking care over raised areas. Allow the grout to set sufficiently before cleaning off any excess with a damp cloth. For areas of mosaic where food is to be prepared, a ready-mixed epoxy grout can be bought, for improved hygienic conditions, to which colour may be added.

A grout can also be made to personal requirements, a useful facility when working on large outdoor mosaics and on works of individual character. Unique textures can be achieved by varying the colour of the sands used, which may be of red, brown, yellow, grey or silver. Wear gloves to mix together four quantities of sand to one quantity of water, and proceed in the following way: create a 'well' in the centre of the mix and add the water slowly. Mix with a trowel to a firm, malleable consistency. For a pool, birdbath or other water container, add a water-based polymer additive to the water before mixing, in the ratio of one volume of water to one volume of the additive; this will reduce to a minimum water permeability in the surface grout.

Opposite page: **Little bird in a gilded frame**
The gold used in the mosaic is extended into the materials used for the simple, wide gold-leaf frame with its inner raised surround.

Three small panels: banana, apple and orange
Each uses a different cement pigment in the grout to accent the coloured tesserae.

Press the grout into the mosaic, making sure all the gaps between the tesserae are filled. Use a damp cloth to clean the surface, and leave under a damp cloth, or cover with polythene, for three days for a really strong set.

CLEANING

Cements with added adhesives are cleaned simply by scrubbing with brushes and cold water. Masonry brushes are used on very large mosaics, and nailbrushes or even toothbrushes are ideal for use on small and intricate mosaics. Sometimes a knife is needed to clean away any stubborn surface adhesive or grout.

Cement-and-sand grouts are cleaned with a solution which contains hydrochloric acid. Branded cleaners can be bought as masonry or patio cleaners. Neat hydrochloric acid must be diluted by adding one part of acid to twenty parts of water. Gloves and protective clothing should always be worn for this procedure. Pour a little of the solution into a plastic or china container, and brush over the mosaic surface; the cement residue will appear to fizz. Wash or hose away with quantities of water before the solution dries, then leave the mosaic to dry naturally.

SEALING

Some mosaics, particularly those made of marble and pebbles, may be protected or enhanced by the addition of a surface sealer. These are brushed onto the mosaic and allowed to dry. Sealers for marble and unglazed tiles can protect the surface from staining and grease while retaining their natural colour; they can also protect porous ceramic mosaic temporarily from water, but may need to be re-applied as required.

Other sealers are used in a mosaic to enhance its natural coloration. A choice of a matt or shiny finish, or a 'wet look' can be used for a variety of effects.

FRAMING

Once a mosaic has been completed and grouted, it may need to be protected or exhibited in a frame. Remember that a frame in effect encloses a mosaic with a finite edge; but a mosaic can just as well be left unframed and given a resin or cement-based edging for protection and finish. Alternatively, mosaics on a wooden support can be framed with greater deliberation, using steel, wood, tiles, mosaic tesserae, aluminium or other metals. Whatever method of framing is decided upon, be certain that it is sympathetic to the design, size, materials and positioning of the mosaic.

HANGING

Many two- and some three-dimensional works can be hung or attached permanently or semi-permanently to a wall. Small wood-based mosaics can be hung as pictures: two screw-eyes or staples can be fixed to the back of the work, then picture wire or steel wire strung between the two, and the work hung from a conventional picture hook or a secure wall fixing.

If the work requires a flat hanging, flush with the wall, two mirror plates can be fitted to the sides or the top and bottom of the work, and screwed into the wall using wall plugs and a drill. The protruding edges of the mirror plates can be disguised to the wall colour if necessary.

Larger works or mirrors on a wooden base, which may be heavy, should have holes pre-drilled and countersunk and should be fixed to the wall before mosaic work commences. They are then taken down to be worked on. Take care to leave adequate space around each drilled hole while working, so you can re-position the work after its completion. Tesserae can be inserted over the holes as permanent or temporary fixtures, depending on whether the mosaic will be relocated in the future. Many mosaics travel with their owners!

With portable 3D mosaics and those made to be hung but having a cement-covered base or armature, the method of hanging to be used should be considered carefully from the outset. Wire or hooks should be inserted into the back of the work whilst it is under construction, because in this way they become integral to the piece and it is assured of a secure hanging feature.

LIGHTING

Mosaics always benefit from careful positioning relative to the amount of daylight they will receive, and the night-lighting available. At night, or in a darkened position, artificial light directed solely onto the mosaic can create a surface of rich complexity. Candlelight is particularly effective on surfaces where gold and other metals, uneven or reflective materials are used. The angles of light and the shadows created by lighting should also be considered, since lighting can enliven or deaden the surface.

During the day, the direction of light from a window, skylight or door can illuminate specific areas of the mosaic – and these may change with the position of the sun or the movement of clouds. This is very apparent on external public murals or garden mosaics where deft angling of materials, or the clever siting of a finished work, can create highly animated mosaics.

10 Author's Work

Mosaic continues to be the author's chosen medium for a very personal mode of self-expression.

The unique properties inherent in all the materials used in making a mosaic provide an endlessly stimulating source with which to explore artistic impulses.

Certain images occur again and again in the work: the tree, the vine, the human figure and the sea, as timeless symbols through which to explore and expound an idea or experience. New themes emerge from time to time and new techniques and materials are experimented with.

Frequent journeys of discovery to the Middle East, India and Europe enable these themes to be continually challenged and questioned within the many differing contexts of light, landscape and culture.

Left: **Lacuna I, 1998, 61x 82cm (24" x 32"), copper gold, alabaster, Carrara marble**
One of a series of two mosaics exploring the possibilities of an area of mosaic bas relief. A contemplative mosaic exploring space, time and loss.

Below: **Every Day I Get the Blues, 1993–5, 43cm x 120 cm (17" x 48"), Venetian white gold, smalti, marble, ceramic, granite, gravel**
One of a series of four mosaics inspired by music and the sea. The mosaic is given a force of direction by a central, horizontal band of granite tesserae.

Above: **Sea Poem I, 1996, 45cm x45 cm (17¾" x 17¾"), granite, antique gold, silver smalti, smalti**
One of two mosaics evoked by contemplating the sea and reflecting on the cycle of life and eternity.

Left: **Oracle, 1998, 41cm x 71cm (16" x 28"), granite, gold, marble, scarabs, silver, smalti, ceramic, vitreous glass, smalti**
The oracle at Siwa, in Eygpt, inspired the creation of the mosaic. A time of questioning and challenging ... for what result?

11 History

ANCIENT BEGINNINGS

The history of mosaic is a long and wondrous one, with periods of great flourishing and expansion, and times of inactivity and misapplication. Historians of mosaic dispute over its real beginnings, and there are controversies and differences of opinion regarding technique, aesthetics and chronology – even over the very word 'mosaic'. It is, however, generally agreed that the earliest appearance of mosaic was in Mesopotamia in the Middle East, where five thousand years ago there existed kingly city-states. One of the oldest was the Sumerian city of Uruq (at the site now known as Warka, in modern Iraq). It was here on the walls of the great city temples that coloured clay cones were used to decorate and strengthen the surface, in much the same way as glass and ceramic tiles do today.

Pieces of stone, mother of pearl and shell were used in the third millennium BC to decorate wooden columns and portable funereal objects, as can be seen in the Standard of Ur, or the Sumerian pillar, at the British Museum in London. Bitumen was used as both adhesive and mortar. The cut pieces had small coils of copper on their backs: these were pushed into this dark bedding, which occasionally rose to the surface, much like a cement mortar might today.

The ancient Egyptians also used stone and tile as imaginative inlays for furniture and walls, and examples can be found in the National Museum of Cairo. There then appears to be a lapse of use, so there is no smooth, continuing development in the making of mosaics.

Opposite page: **The Dance of Salome', baptistery, St Mark's Cathedral, Venice, fourteenth century** The unforgettable image of Salome holding aloft the head of John the Baptist appears more than once on the baptistry walls. The figure is drawn with the simplest of colour variation, relying for effect on a linear profile strongly outlined against a golden background of horizontally laid gold tesserae, in striking contrast to the feathering of the fur trimming.

Left: **Decorated pillars of ancient Uruq (Warka) in Iraq (fourth millennium BC)** The bullet-shaped cones were made of clay about 8cm to 10cm (3in to 4in) long, and were pressed into wet plaster. Their rounded exposed bases were painted in various colours and arranged in lively geometric patterns.

GRAECO-ROMAN MOSAIC

People have used pebbles for paving their floors and walkways right from the beginning of civilization. Pebbles are a readily available, smooth-surfaced material, and their very functional use in making floors with a sound surface would seem a naturally evolving one. Examples of simple geometric designs, using two or three colours and carefully graded pebbles, have been found in the Middle East and the Mediterranean countries since the second and third millennia BC, and it was from these very humble beginnings that mosaic as we recognize it today was born.

At Olynthos on the Chalcidice peninsula in Northern Greece, worn pebble mosaics showing early figurative images with ornamental borders can be found. These fifth-century BC mosaics rely heavily on carpets for their design, and on Greek mythology for their imagery. Figures of lighter colours are placed on darker backgrounds of blue and black. The mortar is allowed to infiltrate between the pebbles so that each one is deliberately defined, the mortar playing an important role in the overall design.

A little later on, in the fourth century BC, pebble mosaics were laid at Eretria in Euboea (Evia), Mostya (Sicily) and more significantly at Pella, the ancient capital of Macedonia, in Greece: the pebble mosaics from King Archelaos's palace in Pella were unearthed in the first half of the twentieth century. They are highly sophisticated, with exquisite floral borders of stalks, tendrils and flowers. The central images are of hunting, and from mythology, and there is also a representation of an 'Amazonomachia' (female warrior). The most skillful pebble floors are by an artist called Gnosis, as we know from an inscription above a stag-hunting scene. He is the oldest-known named 'mosaicist'.

This gradually increasing desire to create an illusion of reality by choosing smaller pebbles to get a close tessellation led to the birth of the mosaic *tesserae* (*tessera*, singular). Originally meaning 'cube' or 'four-sided piece of stone', the word is now used to denote the individual units of material of which a mosaic is made. The tesserae could be made of marble or stone, and the material could be cut and made to fit exactly the shape that was needed.

During the first century BC and thereafter, many floors were made with tesserae of stone, marble and occasionally glass, using Graeco-Hellenic expertise to design and assemble the mosaics. Flourishing centres included Alexandria in Egypt, Sicily in Italy, the island of Delos in Greece, and Pergamum in present-day Turkey. Early designs were based on the

Right: **Stag hunt, detail of hunter, by Gnosis, Pella, Macedonia, Greece, fourth century BC**
Gnosis has used smaller pebbles to create an illusion of muscular strength; some are less than 10mm (⅜in) in diameter and are skillfully contoured to mould the figurative form. Colour is tonal to aid the moulding, with a calculated interplay of light and shade.

concept of carpets or rugs, and were of brightly coloured pieces of marble within tessellated mosaic borders, as seen in the first-century BC mosaics of Aquileia in northern Italy. An example can still be seen from the time of the Emperor Augustine (27 BC–14 AD), of a simple yet beautiful geometric mosaic from the floor of a Roman urban dwelling, with scattered marble fragments in a lively abstract pattern.

The idea of a centralized design being surrounded by a border was at its most sophisticated when the central panel was made independently, away from site, and executed in very finely cut and closely tessellated pieces on raised terracotta trays or marble bases. These were later fixed in place within a previously made border constructed *in situ* of larger-sized and sometimes cruder tesserae. The portable panel, often figurative and executed in *opus vermiculatum* – the small worm-like lines of tesserae – was called an *emblema* (*emblemata*, plural).

Some of the finest works were made by a master mosaicist, or *pictor imaginarius*, called Sosos, from second-century Pergamum. Copies of his works, made in Roman times, have come down to us. He originated the idea of strewing simulated objects on the floor, and making *trompe l'oeil* representations of fish bones, nut shells, lobster claws and other table droppings; these mosaics were given the title *asaroton,* or 'unswept floor'. The original image of 'Drinking Doves at a Bowl' – a mosaic of elaborate interplay of light and shadow reminiscent of a painting – is also attributed to Sosos.

Pompeii was a thriving commercial and agricultural town, with handsome villas built by wealthy owners on the foothills of Mount Vesuvius. The eruption of the volcanic mountain in 79 AD preserved for posterity several fine examples of emblemata, and these give a good idea of the refined Hellenic concepts and workmanship adapted to imperial Roman taste; mosaics were a

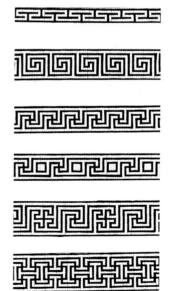

Below: Drawings showing the development and variations of the meander, by Bob Field.

luxury item for paving and flooring at this time. Their vivacity of colour and verisimilitude of imagery is very apparent, and is believed to be directly translated from painting.

The largest known emblema from Pompeii (2.70 x 5.10m) depicts the Battle of Issus. It represents the exact moment between Alexander the Great and King Darius III of Persia when the great king's chariot has turned to retreat and a heroic, wide-eyed Alexander confronts his opponent eye to eye. Basically the mosaic is seen as a supreme masterpiece of mosaic technique imitating a painting, rather than as its essential existence as a mosaic pavement, where illusionistic treatment is unnecessary and denies its material make-up.

Many Hellenic mosaics used motifs of light tone on a dark background. One mosaic depiction of a menu of fish – including squid, mullet, dogfish, and even a murex shell – is executed in the manner of an 'unswept floor', scattered with random placings of objects. The fish are represented realistically, in subtly rendered modulations of light and shade, and are easily identified.

The Greeks also developed a series of motifs that were used in borders and for 'all-over' patterning in floor mosaics; these included meanders, wave crests, key patterns, dentils, chequerboard, swastikas and guilloches. The Romans were intrigued by symmetry and order, and elaborated on these basic geometric designs. Repeated schemes such as grids and interlacing polygons evolved, and it is known that pattern books existed from which designs were copied, suitably scaled up to fit particular sites. The making of complex designs was aided by use of the compass and templates.

Emblemata were costly items for floor decoration, and from around 200 BC, in response to the growing fashion for mosaics, a simpler black-and-white style of mosaic emerged in Italy which lasted until the beginning of the third century. Mosaics using two colours, with cubes of white limestone or marble and black volcanic stone, were more economical to make; the tesserae used were much larger, and backgrounds were often laid more simply in rows of horizontal and vertical lines: the technique known as *opus tessellatum*. Work was also carried out by local workmen on site.

A great number of black-and-white mosaic thresholds (*fauces*) occur in domestic villas at Pompeii, Italy, in the period before the catastrophic eruption of Mt Vesuvius in 79 AD. These include images of dogs, and use black and white and sometimes terracotta red tesserae in *opus tessellatum*. A strong canine image was enough to alert visitors – welcome or unwelcome – of the possible presence inside of such a creature. One such *cave canem* mosaic can be seen in the House of the Tragic Poet, where the animal's fierce teeth warn an intruder to 'beware of the dog'.

The techniques developed, too, from simpler imagery into more complex and original compositions. Thus, rather than appearing as elaborate rugs in a room, mosaics became more architecturally sensitive, often completely filling the floor space. Areas were often very large, since the invention of vaulting allowed for large spans of roof space, and freed up vast areas of floor below that could be decorated completely in all-over patterns in black and white. Numerous floors were decorated in domestic and in public buildings, like baths and *thermae*.

Whereas illusionistic tendencies had been used in the polychromatic Hellenistic emblemata, two-colour usage required new approaches to designing images. Many designers worked with black on white grounds,

often in deliberate silhouette form. Mosaic no longer copied painting, but developed a language of its own that was simpler, bolder and livelier. Imagery, too, became more sensitive to its architectural setting, and to how it was to be viewed within this setting; thus images might reflect the function of the room or building, and depict the occupation of the owner. For example in Ostia, the busy port of Rome, a great many mosaics were made reflecting the city's maritime connections: images of fish and dolphins abound, as well as numerous representations of Neptune, the mythological king of the sea, with his entourage, and other marine activities.

Not only floors, but also walls, vaults and even luxurious ships were decorated during the early Roman period, though very little of this work survives. Exquisite external courtyard mosaics exist in Herculaneum and Pompeii, where grottoes with fountains and walls remain, as well as shrines dedicated to the gods; these *nymphaea* are decorated in stone, glass, pumice and marble chips, as well as with real shells, which were pressed into the mortar to frame the decorated areas or images. The colours are vigorous and strong, and the walls, not needing to be polished smooth like floors, use tesserae

Above: **Black-and-white optical mosaic, Aquileia, Italy, second century AD** A geometric mosaic using optical illusion in preference to figurative illusion in a floor mosaic.

of uneven glass and ridged sea shells. It is from the decorated walls of *nymphaea* that the term *opus musiva*, meaning a wall mosaic, may have come, and from where the very word 'mosaic' may even have originated as the muses were associated with these watery grottoes.

Glass was the favoured material because it is hard-wearing and more impervious than stone to salt air and water; it also creates a colourful and light-catching surface. A good example of its use is the courtyard fountain from the House of the Wise in Pompeii which depicts a grotesque fountain head, framed with shells and large cubes of green glass and marble tesserae.

BRITAIN

The Roman Empire was vast. From about the second century, mosaic schools grew up in each province, and master mosaicists journeyed from one centre to another to work, while pattern books and cartoons were shared and adapted in each country at mosaic workshops, or *officinae*. Each province, however, developed its own individual characteristics, which ranged from flamboyant and polychrome to austere and less colourful.

One of the outposts of Roman domination was Britain, where the earliest known figurative fragments of mosaic were found at Exeter, Isca Dumnoniorum, dating from c. 60 AD. In the first century, black and white, geometric mosaic predominated, as can be seen at Fishbourne palace in Sussex, where fine early geometric floors, consisting of repeating patterns of false cubes, crosses and squares, give the illusion of a three-dimensional surface.

The mosaics were worked *in situ* and much of the material was indigenous:

oolitic limestone and chalk were used for white tesserae, Purbeck marble was used for greys and blues, and sandstone for yellows, reds and brown ochres. Glass mosaic was used only rarely, while imported gold is known in only one instance.

From the second century AD onwards, each *officina* specialized in highly polychromatic imagery, including scenes from Virgil, classical mythology, the four seasons, hunting, and other conventional Roman types. Of particular interest in this context is a mosaic originally from Aldborough (Isurium) in North Yorkshire and now in Leeds City Museum: it depicts the she-wolf with Romulus and his twin brother Remus, the she-wolf being the protector and nurturer of the legendary founders of Rome. The mosaic therefore symbolizes the creation of Rome – and all this from one of Rome's farthest-flung frontiers. Although the style of this third/fourth century (disputed) mosaic is naïve, it is a lively and vigorous realization within a classical framework. The border is geometric with long pointed lozenges in large white, red and black tesserae. It is believed to have been made by local artisans, but shows clearly the extent to which Britain had become Romanized by the fourth century AD.

Another notable fourth century mosaic is from Dorchester (Durnovaria); known as the Hinton St Mary mosaic, it is now in the British Museum. It has a centralized portrait of Christ, which is the earliest known portrayal of Christ in a mosaic pavement. It shows an unbearded fresh-faced young man with deep-set eyes, who wears a Roman-styled tunic and looks like a young emperor; the Christogram, or *chi-rho*, frames his head like rays from a sun. Images of hunting surround this central portrait, but are distanced from it by a

Below: Glossary of motifs; development of the guilloche; Solomon's knot and guilloche mat, by Bob Field.

rich format of patterning using single and double guilloche strands together with a stepped key pattern.

The quality and style of mosaics varied greatly throughout the four centuries of Roman occupation in Britain, but the early fascination for order and exactitude prevailed. There persisted at all times a propensity for geometric motifs that relied on finely crafted workmanship and well trained, industrious and organized teams of workers. A good example is the fourth-century Venus mosaic from Rudston, now in the Hull City Museum: the central figure representing the Roman goddess of love and beauty is of lively provincial interpretation; she is depicted with a mirror (fallen) and an apple, objects which accompany her representation in pavements throughout the Roman world. Here she is seen with a male attendant part human and part fish – an allusion to her first appearance, rising from a sea of foam.

NORTH AFRICA

The workshops of North Africa were both numerous and prosperous. They were strongly Romanized in their imagery of culture and everyday living, but owed much to a rich cross-section of ideas in religious symbolism, where the traditions of the African continent combined with those of Rome, and later on with Byzantium and with Islam. A delightful example is the portrait at El Djem in Tunisia of the goddess Africa, a special divinity who was a cult figure: she is personified with a head-dress of elephant hide featuring an elephant trunk at the apex; her hair is tightly ringletted, as in African dreadlocks, and her skin is in warm ochre tones. Like the gods of Rome, she is centrally placed in the mosaic and surrounded by personifications of the four seasons, tokens of riches and abundance – her power as a religious symbol of worship being thereby fortified.

Left: **Venus mosaic, Rudston, fourth century, Hull City Museum, England (detail)**
A provincial interpretation of the goddess of love and beauty in the central medallion of the mosaic.

Right: **Nilotic scene, detail; Bardo Museum, Tunisia**

Many watery themes occur round the Mediterranean Sea. Here a fisherman protects himself against a toothy hippopotamus, and a crocodile can be seen slinking away. These playful scenes of everyday life are delightfully exuberant, and this high-spirited outlook, typical of the people of North Africa, injects a new vitality into the mosaic medium.

The themes of floors are many, encompassing fertility through the personification of the seasons, and the more abstract quality of time – both cosmic and eternal – through reference to Nature. They also allude to a golden age made possible through the security and munificence of imperial Roman policy. Other popular images are the still lifes of fruits and foods, the 'Xenia' mosaics which were found adorning the floors of the *triclinia* (dining rooms), and the reception rooms of the imperial palaces and villas.

Further imagery related to abundance is that connected with Dionysus; in Tunisia he appears in more than twenty pavements. God of revelry, fertility and wine, he is portrayed along with his Bacchantes, an entourage of satyrs, maenads and other cult followers. The powerful mysteries of the Dionysiac ritual often induced intoxication in the initiates, and the mosaics frequently illustrate this power of fecundity and revelry by a phallic presence, symbolically representing the god Priapus. The pavements of houses were often large and richly decorated, resembling entire tapestries, and in this context Dionysus in his depiction as the god of wine was often surrounded by a complex and colourful design of vine foliage, spread out to cover the floor completely. This type of floor is called *opus musivum*.

Representations of the sea are also common to North African mosaic, sometimes divinized through the image of Neptune, god of the sea, or eternalized through the goddess of beauty, love and protection, Venus. In a mosaic at El Djem, Venus stands, full frontal and naked except for wrist and ankle bangles and a necklace. She has risen from the sea, which is depicted in wavy zigzag tesserae, and holds up her wet locks. Two of her attendant cupids wait upon her, proffering braided ribbons for her hair. The tesserae are of one size in a palette of browns, ochres, terracotta and white in a highly decorated border with rich foliage and linear wave designs.

Above: **Mosaic of the bound Silenus, detail; museum of El Djem, Tunisia**

The mosaic is depicted as a rich, decorative, Dionysian carpet of four entwining vines being harvested by squat, chubby cupids. At the edges, small incidental scenes occur to further engage the viewer: a determined cupid tries to lead a stubborn camel under the eye of a black man, and a ferocious lion tries to frighten a small mouse. Such playful revelry occurs frequently in the mosaics of Roman Africa, and is expressive of the country's abundance and prosperity.

SICILY

The North African influence can be seen in the mosaics of Piazza Armerina in Casale, Sicily, where the richly decorated floor of a luxurious private residence exhibits the same liveliness and *joie de vivre*. Among the images is a female personification of Africa holding an elephant tusk and seated between a striped tiger and a chequered elephant. The floor is vast – about 3,500sq m – and lively in colour and representation: scenes of big-game hunting jostle with playful cupids disporting themselves at chariot racing, spearing rabbits and fishing, most of the themes summarizing the wealthy classes at leisure in the late third and early fourth centuries. The villa was later inhabited during the Byzantine and Arab periods.

Figurative mosaics of similar images abound throughout the Roman provincial Empire, in the Lebanon and Syria and at Antioch (in present-day Turkey), although in these mosaics the treatment is rather more conventional and the borders are more richly conceived and decorated.

JORDAN

The mosaics of Jordan retained and developed a classical interest well into the sixth century and beyond. The earliest truly Graeco-Roman mosaics are found at Gerasa (Jerash) in the north of the country. In the 'Mosaic of the Muses' which held sway from the second to the third centuries, a naturalism prevails in the way the busts of the Muses, the poets and the seasons are depicted, where chromatically shaded tesserae model the features. However, it was during the fifth and sixth centuries at Madaba, south of Jerash, that a different *officina* flourished, both stylistically and technically, in a period that is often termed Jordan's golden age of mosaic making. In this period there was an enduring interest in classical motifs, derived from the pattern books that travelled from one mosaic centre to another – these standardized the imagery throughout the early Byzantine era when Justinian reigned as Emperor in Constantinople. Figurative schemes predominate, amongst them being, most typically, pastoral, hunting and mythological themes.

Classical taste and erudition is most evident in the remarkable mosaic entitled 'The Hippolytus Hall mosaic' at Madaba, in which the Euripidean tale of the ill-fated Phaedra and her beloved Hippolytus is revealed. An original and sensitive chromatic colouring can be observed in the warm but deliberately separate tones of reds, yellows and browns, and there is a beautiful and aesthetic balancing of light and dark backgrounds.

Left: **A nereid (or water nymph), Piazza Armerina, Sicily; third or fourth century**
A follower of the sea-god Neptune, the water nymph sits half draped, regarding her image in a mirror. Beside her sits a tiger, not an obvious native of the island of Sicily: he is brightly striped in tones of warm red, brown and ochre. The sea is represented in short bands of darker tesserae, often placed diagonally – a tradition often found in the mosaics of North Africa.

In a mosaic of Achilles at another Madaba mansion, the technique is more animated, and this deployment can be more simply understood. Though less sophisticated than the Hippolytus Hall mosaic, the Achilles shows a true mosaic interpretation of an idea through stone that is employed for its own sake and not as a painterly vehicle. The figure is linear in style and outlined in darker tesserae; moreover any modulation is linear, and is interpreted through a more stylistic and schematic placing of tesserae. The figure is seen full frontal, a static approach which was to be developed in Europe, particularly in the mosaics of Byzantine Ravenna.

Jordanian mosaics are characterized by inscriptions: these help to date a work and give authorship; many mosaicists, both masters and workers, are known by name. The inscriptions also foretell the history of the early Christian community in Jordan. It is notable that lettering is included as part of an overall design, and is not intrusive

or additional; this foreshadows the inter-relationship between lettering and text in the late Umayyad period when mosaic was used architecturally.

Mosaics in Jordan often featured walled cities and buildings and other such topographical detailing. Madaba itself is best known for the historical map unearthed in 1897. Most mosaic depictions give pictorial views of cities seen from a frontal perspective, in a manner that also occurs in the Madaba map, although to a lesser extent. The larger and more important villages, towns and cities are seen from a bird's eye view.

The style of the map can be dated to the Justinian period (527–565 AD), and it is unique of its kind. It is essentially geographical and topographical, and it is the oldest and most exact map of Palestine before the advent of modern cartography in the early nineteenth century. It is oriented to the east, not the north, and therefore corresponds to the orientation of Christian churches;

Opposite page: **The mosaic of Achilles, Madaba, Jordan, fifth/sixth centuries**
Achilles is naked except for a mantle and a pair of boots (unseen; and covering his vulnerable heels!). He holds a cithara, an early stringed instrument like a lute. An inscription above his head identifies him as the god.

Left: **Jerusalem: detail from the Madaba map, St George's Church, Madaba, Jordan; sixth century**
Jerusalem is depicted as larger than any other city; regarded as the navel of the earth it was the most important Byzantine Christian city. The red lettering on a white ground reads 'The Holy City of Jerusalem'. The city is walled, elliptical in shape with nineteen towers. The plan is much as it appears today, with the Damascus gate on the left, flanked by two towers, in front of an oval square containing a column. A white line of tesserae running from this point down to the Sion gate represents the central colonnaded street

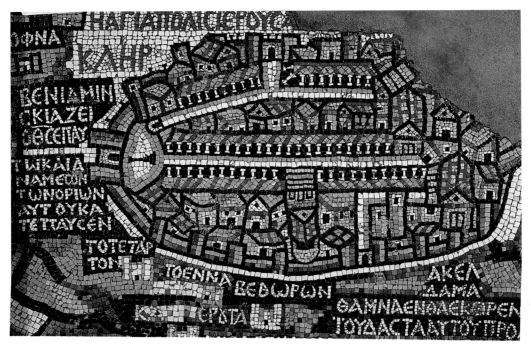

moreover viewers have to imagine themselves looking down from an airborne position above the Mediterranean Sea. The map is not complete, either, but is fragmentary: thus it shows the River Jordan running into the Dead Sea, the Eastern mountains, the Palestine coast down to Ashkelon and Gaza, and the Nile Delta. It is made up of three kinds of representation: a background of deserts, valleys and plains of yellow/white tesserae; mountains, trees and fauna in brown, pink and yellow; and water and rivers in blue, brown and black tesserae.

ISRAEL

The Holy Land of Israel/Palestine yields many mosaics in the Graeco-Roman tradition. Of great interest are

pavements of Jewish synagogues of the Byzantine period. One near a Roman spa in Hammath Tiberius incorporates pagan, Christian and Jewish symbolism.

The iconography of early Christian mosaics imbued with pagan imagery evolved quite naturally with new symbolic and allegorical reference; thus pagan motifs such as cupids become winged angels or putti, and a fight between a turtle and a cock becomes a symbolic eternal struggle between the dark and the light. The symbol of the peacock, which can be seen on a fourth-century floor at Heptapegon (Tabgha), north-west of the Sea of Galilee in Israel, portrays everlasting life through alliance with the new religion of Christianity. Further scenes on the floor depict the flora and fauna of a typical marshy landscape: Nilotic geese, ducks and lotus plants.

Right: **The mosaic of Hammath Tiberius, Israel; fourth century** Helios/Apollo, the sun god, is at the centre of the pavement: he was generally identified with the reigning emperor. He is depicted with his hand raised in benediction, an allusion to his universal power and veneration, as symbolized by the orb that he holds in his other hand; this posture was to be absorbed into the Christian repertoire. Surrounding him are zodiac symbols from pagan Rome, identified by Hebrew script. An upper panel leads into an area where the Torah Ark would be placed, and is totally Jewish in imagery. Centrally positioned is a representation of the Ark flanked by the *menorah* or ʿn-branched ʿk, and other ʿ Jewish ʿ identity.

THE EARLY BYZANTINE PERIOD

With the rise and spread of Christianity the art of mosaic flourished, quickly recognized as being an ideal medium to illustrate the new philosophy. A majestic and monumental art form was needed to proclaim the new faith, and so the Byzantine emperor, Justinian, was among the first to encourage the arts into Ravenna, the new capital of his empire. From the early fifth century, the capital had been transferred from Milan to Ravenna, a move that had prompted the construction of a great number of new churches, baptisteries, mausoleums and other religious buildings.

The new religion was to be seen in a different light. No longer were the precious symbols to be trodden underfoot: they were to be raised to cover the walls, vaults, apses, naves and domes of the new edifices, and so materials such as glass, semi-precious stones and mother-of-pearl were employed to give scintillating and radiant effects. The one which came most into its own was glass: an opaque and richly coloured glass called smalti, together with a glass that held gold and silver leaf. These two materials significantly changed the way in which mosaics were observed and applied.

RAVENNA

In its design and decor the Byzantine church represented the early mediaeval concept of the church as an image of the cosmos. It had a fixed pictorial canon which prescribed a hierarchical arrangement of persons according to their importance – and nowhere is this more fully depicted than in the two panels on the apsidal wall of the church of San Vitale in Ravenna (mid-sixth

century). In one panel the Empress Theodora is depicted together with her attendants, offering a golden chalice.

Opposite the panel of the empress is a mosaic of the Emperor Justinian offering a golden paten, or plate. As the representative of Christ on earth, he is centrally placed with his attendant dignitaries. The figures are front facing with little attempt at portraiture: they seem disembodied, as if inhabiting another realm – not of this world, but of the spirit; they appear to be in a contemplative state, demanding the same of the viewer. To enhance this effect the mosaics show no attempt to create depth by shading or modelling.

They have a sumptuous richness and beauty. Glass smalti is used for its maximum chromatic appeal, and tesserae are angled into the mortar to produce an uneven multi-tone surface so that the play of light will give a sense of movement. This dematerializes the surface, disassociating the image from any illusion of reality; it also gives the mosaic a sense of non-attachment to its actual fixed and permanent placing within an architectural setting.

There were gradual developments in

Below: **Baptistry of the cathedral, Ravenna, Italy, fifth century**
The mosaics of the Neonian baptistry or *illuminatorium*, a building for spiritual enlightenment, are in complete empathy with the architectural setting, an ornately decorated octagonal structure with a vaulted dome. A medallion which depicts the baptism of Christ lies at the centre of the dome, the imagery moving downwards in concentric bands to the eight corners of the spandrels separating each window. The figures of the apostles and the vertical pillar imagery span the interior of the dome and lead the eye to the image of the baptism.

Above: **The three Magi/kings, detail, St Apollinare Nuovo, Ravenna, Italy, sixth century**
Detail from one of the two processional mosaics that run the entire length of the nave, the artist obviously delighting in the uses of richly warm colour and pattern.

how background was depicted, and Ravenna saw them all: the white ground favoured by the Romans on their floors changed to blue for celestial representations, and green for pastoral ones, and by the sixth century a gold ground came to dominate, as can be seen in the richly lustrous processional mosaics at St Apollinare Nuove.

In the previously mentioned portrait of the Empress Theodora her golden halo or nimbus uses the colour red to distinguish it from its uniformly golden ground, and also a line of angled silver tesserae; this procedure was to be more fully developed in the eleventh century.

Natural stone is used to represent flesh, its soft non-reflecting surface contrasting with the brilliant and light giving surface of the glass smalti. Marble is also used to delineate between areas of similar colour, and mother of pearl is used for the empress's jewelled diadem.

BYZANTIUM / CONSTANTINOPLE / ISTANBUL

Early Byzantine influence is seen in Hagia Sophia, the patriarchal church of Byzantium (formerly Constantinople, now present-day Istanbul); this church was the greatest monument to imperial munificence and artistic influence in the sixth century. Built by Constantine after he transferred the imperial seat from Rome to Constantinople in 330 AD, the church was embellished by Justinian in the sixth century. Its immense size and impressive but plain exterior belies its light and exalted interior. Inside, the eye is directed to an expansive dome lit by a circular band of windows which filter the incoming light onto a golden mosaic surface, thereby giving the illusion of continual movement. Only a few sixth-century mosaics survive in Hagia Sophia to give testimony to the increasing use of mosaic throughout the early Byzantine period, when the medium achieved its highest potential.

THE SPREAD OF BYZANTINE INFLUENCE

The Byzantine empire spread eastwards to Syria and Israel, and on into Egypt, where the monastery of St Catherine is one of Justinian's most impressive foundations; its remote setting on Mount Sinai helped to preserve many icons, artefacts and mosaics which would otherwise have fallen prey to the hands of the later iconoclastic emperors. During intermittent periods in the eighth and ninth centuries, countless works of art were destroyed in the lands under their control.

In the 'Mosaic of the Transfiguration' in the apse of St Catherine's monastery at Mount Sinai, Egypt, the morning light from the east windows enhances the white clothing of the figures in an impressively composed mosaic. Rows of silver tesserae emanating from the central figure of Christ are angled both towards and against the light, giving a surface symbolic of celestial iridescence

and creating a play of light expressive of divinity. Byzantine influence is apparent also in the decorative mosaic interiors of the Dome of the Rock in Jerusalem, and the Great Mosque of Damascus. Between 632 AD when the Prophet Muhammad died, and 647 AD, the Arab caliphs created a new Arab Muslim empire, and a vast area encompassing Iraq, Syria, Iran, Egypt and Palestine – much of which had previously been the empire of Byzantium – came under one rule.

The earliest pictorial representations of this new Islamic civilization are on the interior walls of the Dome of the Rock, built in 691. The large cupola,

Below: **Decorative elements from the Great Mosque at Cordova, in Spain**
Leaf and lotus forms, palmettes and trefoils, are some of the motifs which can be seen in the rich Hispano/Umayyad mosaic decoration on the façade of the *mihrab* in Cordova, Spain, from the tenth century onwards under the caliphate of Al-Hakam II.

spandrels and the soffits of the ambulatories around the rocky outcrop upon which the great church is built are covered with highly decorative glass tesserae, and in the extensive use of gold, semi-precious stones, mother-of-pearl and gold smalti, a sense of rich opulence is powerfully conveyed. Also, the classical art forms transformed into Byzantine ornate design are very much apparent: scrolls, vases, cornucopias, trees and leaves are depicted alongside images from pre-Islamic Syria and Iran – for example, the bud-like flower form in various shades of blue and green. Again, the splendour of the mosaic lies in the association of ideas it represents, in this case proclaiming the rich bounties, spiritual and earthly, to be obtained by adhering to such a religion.

From 661 the capital of this new empire moved to Damascus in Syria. Under the Umayyad Caliphate, the great Mosque of Damascus was constructed, the interior of which was again decorated with richly chromatic mosaics of green, blue, red, gold and silver. The mosaics are rigid, and without figurative or animal forms, and continue the repertoire of late classical antiquity and early Byzantine motifs – vegetal, floral and architectural.

During the eighth century, one branch of the Umayyad family fled from uprisings in Syria to Europe, and in Spain founded the emirate of Cordova; stylistically this was to flourish in the ensuing Hispano-Moresque art of Andalusia, where Syrian forms are even today clearly to be seen in the jewel-like *mihrab* or sanctuary of the Mosque of Cordova. Here, the magnificence of the Hispano/Umayyad repertoire of motifs is shown to glittering perfection within a decorative marble framework.

GOLD

Gold was first used in Rome to simulate a supernatural light: it can be found in a mosaic from the necropolis of St Peter's in Rome, in the third century. Christ is depicted as an Apollo/sun god riding his chariot, and concentric bands of gold tesserae in the *nimbus*/halo radiate from his head. This is the first known instance where gold is made to simulate divine light emanating from and surrounding a divine figure.

This usage spread throughout the early Byzantine world, and gold came to predominate in all-over background coverage where previously heavenly blue and Elysian green had dominated. Silver was also used, but mainly to avoid any devaluation of gold through excessive use; this is particularly the case when a golden halo is depicted on a uniformly golden ground. Tesserae were

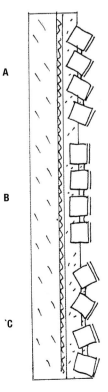

Regular and irregular placing of tesserae.

A: uniformly angled gold tesserae
B: unangled gold tesserae
C: randomly angled gold tesserae

also tilted at extreme angles, either uniformly to obtain conforming shades of gold or randomly to create a broken and variously hued golden surface.

Gold was also used for purely decorative reasons: to model the light in drapery or jewellery, or to pick out detailing in architectural renderings. It was further used to replicate the appearance of pure gold in vases, jugs and drinking vessels, as in the mosaics in the fourth-century vault of Santa Constanza in Rome, and the fourth-century Chresis mosaic from Antioch, where Chresis offers jewels and golden crowns made of golden smalti.

THE MIDDLE BYZANTINE PERIOD

In contrast to the artistic flowering of the early Byzantine period, the influence of which spread widely throughout Europe and the Near and the Middle East, there followed a time when few significant mosaics were made – this was during the iconoclastic disruption which took place between the eighth and the tenth centuries. Only after the restoration of the Holy Roman Empire in 800 AD and a general amelioration of the situation in the Byzantine empire was there a slow and gradual renewal of interest in religious art for church interiors.

GREECE

The church of Hosios Lukas in Phocis, Greece, was richly endowed with mosaics in the early twelfth century and seemed to initiate a second flowering of mosaic work. The interior is completely faced with mosaics which follow an orthodox decorative system with a strict iconographic programme, and a veritable gallery of portraits crowds the

walls: of saints, prophets, bishops and Christ himself in his role as Redeemer. The visual cycle is topped by the mosaic of the dome, which is an effigy of Christ at his most omnipotent, the Pantocrator. The style is serious yet gentle, and has an overall ascetic sense.

At Daphni, too, a complete and wonderful programme of mosaics can be seen, depicting scenes from Christ's life: the Annunciation, the Nativity, the Baptism and the Transfiguration – an even wider iconographic programme than at Hosios Lukas. The nave, narthex and vestibule are completely covered, and there is a new nobility to be seen: a re-observing of the classical heritage. As a result the mosaic demonstrates a

Above: **An angel, the monastery of Daphni, Greece, eleventh/twelfth century**
A classically drawn elegance combined with a new tenderness can be seen in this depiction of an angel. The modelling of the features and the styling of the hair also hint at a certain mannerism, the figure being less vigorous and expressive than some of the earlier mosaics of Ravenna.

successful balancing of pose, a harmony of silhouetted outline, and a studied arrangement of drapery, all combined with supreme draughtsmanship. This was a new stylistic elegance overlaid with a new humanity.

SICILY

The frescoes and mosaics of the Sicilian churches at Palermo, Cefalú and Monreale were to imitate this resurgent Byzantine style.

At Monreale the cathedral's whole interior is coated with mosaics: they glisten with light and dazzle the visitor on entering. It is a grand and unifying creation – vast, spacious, balanced and illuminating. Isolated scenes and figures are placed within large interconnecting areas of golden background. The mosaics have renounced the purity of colour, and any modelling of outline or robing is picked out with white or muted tones of tesserae; there is no chromatic blending as in the earlier Byzantine period. Gold is made to outshine colour, and colour is therefore attuned to the gold: gold dominates and the colours do not resonate with each other.

THE LATE BYZANTINE PERIOD

Venice
The mosaics that cover the interior and the exterior of the great edifice of St Mark's Cathedral in Venice span the period from the eleventh to the fifteenth centuries. The cycle adorning the atrium describes a series of historical and religious happenings taken from the Old Testament, and was inspired by the mosaics in Sicily. The creation myth was quite in vogue at the time, and religious decoration throughout Europe

was depicting the story in stained glass and manuscripts, particularly in France and England. The episodes represented here are of Adam and Eve, the tower of Babel, Noah and the Flood, and the lives of Moses, Joseph and Abraham.

Rome
In Rome, too, there was a flowering of mosaic application, the designs often combining the decorative elegance of the imagery of the period with a deep theological reflection. For example, the inspiration for the apsidal mosaic of the twelfth-/thirteenth-century church of San Clemente is based on the incarnate nature of Christ and redemption through the Cross, and the imagery which represents this divine plan for the salvation of humanity centres on a vine spiralling outward in ever-increasing scrolls and linked to a central image of a cross. The whole work is a riot of coloured tesserae and stone, a joyous, dynamic and vigorous expression of the energy of the message.

Istanbul
In a splendid finale to Byzantine art, there was a return to intense colour-blending. This is most clearly demonstrated at the monastery of Chore, now the Kariye Museum, in Istanbul, Turkey where the mosaic panels are richly polychromatic and sumptuous on a scintillating multi-golden background. The spandrels of the narthex describe the life of Mary the Virgin like a richly illustrated picture book; she is depicted as a blue-clad figure, her golden halo framing a benignly drawn face.

MOSAIC FLOORS

The early Graeco-Roman tradition of mosaic paving continued into the

Opposite page: **The apse, San Clemente, Rome, twelfth/thirteenth century**
The vine is, in reality, an acanthus emanating from the ground. Symbolically it is watered by divine blood and s p i r a l s in increasing profusion to encompass and nourish the whole of mankind, thus revitalizing the enduring imagery of the Vineyard of the Lord.

Paleo-Christian era, and good examples can be seen on the richly symbolic floors at Aquileia and nearby Grado in northern Italy; these date from the fourth to the sixth centuries. The images of fish are now known to be not only decorative observances, but representations of Christ himself; the Greek word *ictys* being formed from the initial letters of '*Iesos Christos Theou Uios Soteer*', meaning 'Jesus Christ, Son of God, Saviour'.

OPUS TESSELLATUM AND *OPUS SECTILE*

Many later Christian churches and cathedrals drew on the rich geometric and pagan imagery of earlier times to carpet the floors of their basilicas with mosaic designs which were to be interpreted within a newly understood context. Two techniques were used for the decoration: *opus tessellatum* or true mosaic, and *opus sectile*, and they were used separately, together, and alternating with each other.

On the whole, true tessellated floors, made with cut tesserae of coloured marble, were used to expound the figurative imagery of Christianity: for example animals in combat represented good over evil, Christian over pagan; and birds, particularly peacocks, were used as symbols of eternal life, as the flesh of the bird was understood never to perish. *Opus sectile*, an inlay technique of geometric patterning, used marble and coloured stone cut into recognizable shapes – triangles, squares, rhomboids and solid circles – to create highly coloured, intricate and sometimes optical floors, often inspired by oriental carpets and fabrics. This technique was perfected by master craftsmen of the fourteenth and fifteenth centuries.

Wonderful examples of both techniques in conjunction can be seen in Venice on the floor of the cathedral of San Marco, and at SS Maria e Donato on the island of Murano in the Venetian

Right: **Detail of fish in the basilica at Aquileia in northern Italy, dating from the fourth century**
A symbolic detail from the floor mosaic which is 750sq m in total. The pavement of the nave of the cathedral is a vast and eloquent testament to the accomplishments of the early Paleo-Christian mosaic artists.

lagoon, where mosaic images of trees, paired crickets (!) and eagles are surrounded by marble tesserae cut into triangles, circles and rectangles.

INTARSIA WORK

This is a related inlay technique with a smooth surface. The visible support, which is also the base, may be made of wood, metal, stone or ivory; whilst the decoration, most commonly of semi-precious stones or marble, is cut and laid into this.

COSMATI WORK: *OPUS ROMANUM*

In the thirteenth and fourteenth centuries the art of mosaic declined, and was superseded to a certain extent by painting and sculpture; however, before this decline really took hold, a new form of mosaic-type work developed for floors from the end of the twelfth century. Known as 'Cosmatine', or '*Cosmati*', it was a highly decorative technique composed primarily of geometric shapes (squares and triangles); it was of Arab origin and in fact came from Sicily, where intricate inlays of glass and stone were used architecturally as repeating patterns.

In Rome, the Cosmati family developed the technique and used it in cloisters, pulpits and portals, and also in wondrous floors of complex pattern and design: in these, exotic marbles and stone were cut into repeating motifs of geometric shapes and laid within bands of marble, forming interconnecting designs, often with initial bands of solid porphyry or serpentine; the central medallion was sometimes cut from an antique marble column. The surface was then grouted and ground, and finally polished to a smooth finish.

There is a fine example of such work in Westminster Abbey in London, cut from green porphyry and Purbeck marble, carried out by Odoricus and dating from 1268.

THE DECLINE OF MOSAIC

From the thirteenth and fourteenth centuries, new aesthetic values were appearing in the art world, centred in Italy. These values were not concerned with the metaphysical concepts and symbolism which had imbued Byzantine religious expression, and to which the medium of mosaic was ideally suited, but were concerned with an emerging humanism. The relationship between man and God, and man and Nature was being questioned, and a new and visual interpretation was needed – a Renaissance. Painting and painters, much encouraged by Giorgio Vasari (1511–74), an art critic, historian and painter of the High Renaissance period, began to recreate nature through reason, using laws of perspective and mastering techniques such as *sfumato* and *chiaroscuro* to create a believable, naturalistic and ordered world. Such virtuosity led to the raising of the artist's status to a new, elite position, and mosaic was relegated to an artisan's occupation: his expertise, previously so highly acclaimed, was now reserved for no more than the restoration and repair of bygone works, or to translate renowned paintings from cartoons or from the finished works into stone and glass. This was defined by Domenico Ghirlandaio as '*la vera pittura per l'eternita*', meaning true painting for eternity.

Mosaic's subservience to painting resulted in an enormous increase in the

Above: **Detail, Cosmati work at S. Maria Maggiore, Rome, Italy**
A superb example of the work of the Cosmati family, where colour and pattern appear in bold contrast in a richly controlled floor design.

and development at the Vatican Workshop, of spun smalti, or *smalti filati*: in this process a single glass cube was heated and stretched into a thread-like form of minute circumference, then cut into tiny pieces for use in table inlays, pictures and furniture – thus pandering to the refined tastes of the wealthy and those who required souvenirs from Italy on their return from the Grand Tour.

PRE-COLUMBIAN AZTEC

The unparalleled decorative quality of mosaic had been recognized by the peoples of Peru and Mexico since the first millennium BC. Portable objects such as shields, masks, pectorals and even skulls were encrusted with randomly sized tesserae of bone, shell, gold and turquoise, considered the most precious of stones, and were then used in rituals and as ceremonial regalia.

In the capital of the Aztec empire of pre-Columbian America, now present-day Mexico, the tradition of mosaic decoration continued into the sixteenth century. After the Spaniard Cortés had reconquered the area, many of the treasures were brought to Europe and found their way into the collections of the Medici and the Vatican.

A ritual shield of the Mixtec/Aztec period (1400–1500) can be seen at the British Museum in London. The tree, the serpent and the golden disc are all symbols, part of the rich metaphysical imagery of the Aztec culture: the disc represents the navel of the earth, and the serpent, when worn ceremonially by warrior kings or priests, reaffirmed their powerful position as mediators in the world between the outer cosmic layers of heaven and the earth – this established beyond all question their authoritative rights.

quantities of coloured smalti needed to emulate the inexhaustible colour palette of an oil painter. During the sixteenth and into the eighteenth and nineteenth centuries, the Vatican mosaic workshop produced in excess of 27,000 colours.

A further misapplication of the art of true mosaic occurred during the eighteenth century when mosaics made of minute glass tesserae were used to produce jewellery and pictures with the finest detailing and colouring. This practice was initiated by the Vatican Workshop, established in 1576, at Rome in Italy. The second half of the century witnessed a further invention

MID-NINETEENTH CENTURY/VICTORIAN

The art of mosaic was revitalized in the mid-nineteenth century when a Venetian glass-maker, Lorenzo Radi, together with his patron, the Venetian lawyer Antonio Salviati, devised a method for making and transporting mosaic to meet the needs of a North European industrial civilization. This involved making up large-scale mosaic schemes in the workshops of Venice and putting them onto a temporary backing paper in the reverse or indirect technique. The finished products were then shipped to their destinations and were fixed on site. Decorative schemes were made for the Louvre and the Opéra in Paris, and Westminster Cathedral and the Albert Memorial in Victorian England.

This way of working may have reduced material and labour costs, as the glass was made industrially in uniform size and of standardized colours, but it also compromised the true character of mosaic because the smooth surface, which was a requirement for the prefabricated technique, lost much of its lively light-reflecting surface appeal. The resulting mosaics were therefore often characterless and academic.

THE LATE NINETEENTH/ TWENTIETH CENTURIES

Exploratory progress in the late nineteenth and early twentieth century in painting was to open an exciting and experimental way forward for mosaic. Artists of the Art Nouveau period with their preference for a decorative style characterized by flat shapes and free-flowing lines were attracted to mosaic for its obviously ornate appeal derived from its exotic inheritance.

One such artist, Gustav Klimt (1862–1918), an Austrian painter, developed a personal style which owed much of its rich, ornate innovation to observation and study of the Byzantine mosaics of Ravenna. He incorporated mosaic into his work alongside painted areas and purposefully unique enamelled ceramics. The mosaics he made for the dining room of the Palais Stoclet in Brussels, Belgium, were exotic, chromatic and refined, and much suited to the tastes of the wealthy pre-war Brussels magnate.

Another artist of the period who was to have a far-reaching impact on many later generations was Antonio Gaudí (1852—1926). Tiles were a natural product of Spain and a legacy from its Hispano-Moresque background, and by way of experiment Gaudí had used tiles for external decoration from very early on in his architectural career. It was a cheap and easily procured material, and it features in many of his buildings, including Casa Vicens, Casa Milá and most inventively in the serpentine park bench of the Parc Güell, part of a

Below: **Vatican workshop, Rome, Italy**
A mosaicist at work on a portative mosaic relying for its design on a cartoon or photostat. Easel mosaics may be original or translations of a painting. Today the workshop primarily carries out restoration and miniature work.

virtuoso scheme commissioned by his benefactor Count Güell.

In 1889 Antonio Gaudí saw a display panel made by Angelo Orsoni for the Universal Exhibition in Paris, which showed samples of the gold and glass smalti range, demonstrating perfectly their exquisite coloration and virtuosity. He was immediately persuaded into using smalti alongside glazed tiles for his wondrously original creation in Barcelona, the church of the Sagrada Famiglia.

Mosaic had therefore broken loose from interior restraint with its dependency on expensive gold and glass, and, as in the *nymphaea* of Herculaneum, was once again being used in an exterior setting and incorporating material of the locality.

MID-TWENTIETH CENTURY

During the 1950s Mexican artists were to draw on their pre-Columbian history to instill a new national identity for the country within a socialist doctrine. Art works were created as painted and mosaic murals which incorporated a social, political or economic theme in large, colourful, often figurative statements on the walls of institutions, theatres and universities, or as sculptural works for public amenities such as the central Mexican waterworks. They were constructed mostly of indigenous materials: tiles, glazed ceramics and local stone. The artists involved with creating these large pieces were Diego Rivera, Juan O'Gorman, José Chavez Morado, José Clemente Orozco, and David Alfaro Siqueiros, along with others dedicated to the socialist ideal.

Many artists of the mid-twentieth century worked at some time with mosaic to explore its values and potential as a medium. Pablo Picasso, whose cartoons were executed by Hjalmar Boyesen, took his inspiration from film strips and animation; Fernand Léger designed mosaics for two sites in France, the Assy project to rejuvenate sacred art, and the façade for his museum in Biot; and Marc Chagall did many drawings for mosaic work which were made up in Italy, including twelve 'fragments' for the floors of the Knesset (the parliament) building in Jerusalem, depicting the twelve tribes of Israel.

Oscar Kokoschka, like those artists previously mentioned, had paintings translated into mosaics in Italy, continuing the fifteenth-century creed of making mosaic 'paintings for eternity' – which, however expertly made, lose something of their initial vitality and spontaneity. A popularizing of mosaic making was witnessed in the 1950s and 1960s when a great many lamp bases and ashtrays were made and given a mosaic veneer by enthusiastic followers of mosaic; these were often quite decorative, but their makers failed to energize or understand the true power and potential of the material.

Artists who were finding a real balance between the initial design and the finished object were those who both designed and executed their own work, and who had an intimate knowledge of each tessera and its position in the work. In Italy an artist of the Cubo-Futurist school, Gino Severini (1883–1966), found inspiration in the Byzantine mosaics at Ravenna, seeing in their formal and more abstract qualities similarities with what he and his contemporaries were trying to achieve in their work. He explored form through juxtaposing planes of different shapes and colour in the rich tones of Venetian smalti.

Much of Severini's life was spent exploring the techniques of mosaic within a painterly context but with full understanding of the material, its light effects and colour resonance; this interest and ability is reflected in many delightful, small still-life mosaics made between 1930 and 1960.

In this series he created images with rich, multi-faceted surfaces, exploring the forms of the objects and their relationship to each other on a two-dimensional surface. He initiated and founded two schools of mosaic, one in Paris, and one in Ravenna: the latter is the Instituto Statale d'Arte per il Mosaico 'Gino Severini' (the mosaic Institute of Gino Severini), which continues to have an impressive line-up of teachers and students of great skill and originality. He made many mosaics, large and small, public and private, his enthusiasm for the subject leading him to teach in Paris and lecture in Ravenna. A theme that he constantly stressed was the importance of integrating the art of designing with the art of making.

In England, the Russian émigré Boris Anrep (1885–1969) worked tirelessly not only to create many large and impressive works in mosaic using the reverse technique, but also to elucidate through lectures the qualities of the mosaic medium. He found its permanence, coloration, hardness and reflective qualities admirably suited to the decorating of buildings constructed of equally durable and exciting materials, namely brick, stone and glass. His subjects were often contemporary, portraying prominent figures of the day in allegorical settings. Edith Sitwell and Bertrand Russell appear as 'Sixth Sense' and 'Lucidity' in the virtuoso floor of the National Gallery in London. A mosaic of 1922 shows 'Moments in the Life of a Lady of Fashion', in nine variously shaped mosaic panels of flat, angular design, admirably indicative of an exuberant post-war 'cultured' class.

The American artist Jeanne Reynal (born 1903), who had earlier been an assistant to Boris Anrep both in England and in France, returned to the United States in search of a personal style for her work. She explored an uneven setting surface and the physicality of the tesserae, always emphasizing their qualities whether they were constructed of semi-precious stones, smalti or vitreous glass. After much experimenting, she arrived at a very loose and highly personal style in which, like the action painters of the period, she sprinkled her material – coloured mother-of- pearl, and glass

Above: **Detail of a gable spandrel on the Albert Memorial in London, England, dating from the 1860s**
A small spandrel flanking the allegorical figure personifying painting, designed by John Clayton and George Bell, and executed by Salviati and his company.

Above: **Park Güell, detail, Barcelona, Spain, by Antonio Gaudi, 1907–1912.** Shaped of pre-fabricated pieces, these vertical forms create an extraordinary structure, a sculptural barrage incorporating glazed tiles in a collage of colour and decorative texture.

image of the mural, continuing their collective interest in mosaic collage.

The Naïves

Other artists active at the time were working in complete isolation and ignorance of the works of their renowned contemporaries, or indeed of the works of Byzantium: these were known as the Naïves.

In the south of France, at Hauterives, a postman termed Facteur Cheval (1836–1924) created in his garden a fantastic palace of columns, figures, pinnacles and stairways out of found and collected stones and rocks: the Palais Idéal. It was begun in 1879 and finished in 1912, and was the conceit of an ordinary man with an extraordinary vision – the more so since the finished work incorporates a world harmony of thought and religion.

Among the many natural creators who collect and create with no knowledge of artistic world events is a Russian, Bodan Litnanski (born 1920), who as a prisoner of war was repatriated into France. His house and garden in Viry Noureuil are encrusted with recycled débris, strung, hung and kept together by cement. Every imaginable item of rubbish is there – toys, dolls, stones, shells, bottles, metals, glass and bricks – all carefully and personally chosen with a logic and order that connects one material with another into a mosaic of discarded delights.

Also in France, at Chartres, another extraordinary man, Raymond Isidore (born 1900), a grave digger, was making his simple self-built house into his entire world by covering every conceivable surface with images of his wife, family, animals and flora, out of china and porcelain. Inside his home, beds, cupboards, chairs, the sewing machine and even the radio, have a skin of bright ceramic mosaic. Outside, the

and stone – over a base of white cement coloured with pigment, often in pastel shades. The tesserae were finally tapped into permanent positions to create two-dimensional and free-standing mosaics of spontaneity, light and delight.

In England the artist Hans Unger was creating mosaics with his assistant Eberhard Schultze; these were mostly abstract, and integrated collage and mosaic into designs in which the dynamics of the shapes and overall forms were stressed and a balanced composition made.

Further works by Unger and Schultze also include materials relevant to the

Above: **Still life with lobster by Gino Severini, 1951 (50 x 70cm)**
A small still life using smalti as facets of colour to explore volume and space on a
two-dimensional plane.

Penguin Books canteen mural, Harmondsworth, London, England, 1964
The mural was designed in green, turquoise and orange, representative of the colours of Penguin paperbacks. The wall is constructed in disguised panels, and is like a bas-relief with tesserae of varying size and height, The whole is made uniquely relevant by the insertion of printing blocks, linotype pages and type face.

tool shed, the courtyard walls, the paving and flowerpots have a further incrustation of polychrome ceramic fragments. All the material was painstakingly collected from the tips and waste-bins of the great city.

From the age of thirty until his death in 1964 Isidore – aptly named '*Pique-Assiette*' ('plate-picker') from Picassiette (little plate) – worked obsessively on his home environment; he had no formal art training, and his only artistic motivation was the delight he found in the material and in the joy of creating. In the inner courtyard of La Maison Picassiette, stands a 'black' stone throne from where Pique-Assiette contemplated his world. It incorporates many images of Chartres cathedral, an ever-present reminder of

his own uniquely personal divine source of inspiration.

Sri Nek Chand Saini (born 1924) is another untutored master of creativity, his work of art being the Rock Garden in Chandigarh, near New Delhi in India. It is a creation of inspiration and pure genius, one man's concept realized in collaboration with a changing team of workers. Of enormous size – twenty-five hectares and still growing – the garden is peopled with over five thousand sculptures, linked by walkways and interconnecting arches leading through courtyards, grottoes, palaces and naturally evolving spaces. The idea originated with Nek Chand's compulsion to make a kingdom – there is a throne – and to incorporate within it his vision of

India: dancers, hookah smokers, holy men, animals, peacocks, beggars, water carriers ... the list is seemingly endless, and likewise their interpretation.

The land and the materials are reclaimed: the materials include crockery, household sanitary ware, water pots, colourful bangles, bottle tops, glass and much industrial refuse. All is cut by hand with stones and the simplest of tools, yet as sensitively as precious Venetian gold and smalti.

The impact of the garden is not just one of tremendous originality and size; the repeated, and yet individualized sculptures create a huge impact *en masse*, alongside great intimacy and individuality, just like life. The effect is total — an experience of enormous absurdity and profundity.

Simon (Sabato) Rodia (1879–1965), an Italian-born American, was yet another untutored creator who used the medium of mosaic to embellish his extraordinary works in a run-down area of Los Angeles in America. The compulsion to make something big — very big — was the motivation behind a work that spanned thirty-four years. It consists of an elaborate and instinctively worked-out network of pavilions and labyrinths connecting a series of towers — cones of spiralling, concrete-covered steel one hundred feet high. The surfaces are covered with an intricate and inventive pattern of sparkling fragments of bottle glass, shells, rocks and stones. It has been estimated that 6,000 pieces of coloured bottle glass, 15,000 glazed tiles, 10,000 sea shells, 11,000 pieces of crockery and many hundreds of telephone line insulators and mirrors were used in the work, demonstrating the extraordinary virtuosity of a single-handed, and single-minded creator.

This natural inner compulsion to make things, in a persistent and

indefatigable way, and sometimes under the most restrictive conditions of space and materials with no obvious rationale except that of the inner voice, is a common denominator among the naïve artists who 'create' regardless of an audience or training. One who works in a naïve manner but who moves within exalted artistic circles is Niki de Saint Phalle (born 1930 in France). Her Giardino dei Tarocchi, or Tarot Garden, in Capalbio in southern Tuscany, was inspired by a visit to Barcelona in 1955 to see the Parc Güell of Antonio Gaudí. Her homage is duly acknowledged in the garden in an arcaded circular courtyard

Above: **Le Palais Idéal, detail, dating from 1879, by postman Cheval Hauterives, France.** Part of the extraordinary composite work which incorporates a Khmer temple, a mosque, a Hindu sanctuary, a feudal castle, a Swiss chalet, the manger at Bethlehem — and here, the Three Kings.

Above: **General view of the Rock Garden (detail), Chandigarh, India, in the 1960s**
The earliest phase of the Rock Garden, the kingdom of Nek Chand Saini. Figures, birds and animals populate the vast space surrounded by trees grown from seeds planted at the same time as their creation.

of colour, reminiscent of that beneath the Serpentine Bench.

The garden contains twenty-two sculptures, symbols from the Major Arcana of this oldest of card games. Smaller sculptures were made in polyester resin; larger sculptures have a steel frame covered by wire mesh which is then sprayed with gunite cement: finally they are covered with a variety of ceramics, glass and mirrors of extreme colour variation and vivacity. To end with, the effect is one of walking through a garden of mystery, and of intense colour and light and magic. The personality of the garden – formerly a quarry in the densely green hillside – and the interpretation of the ancient symbols, sometimes accompanied by scratched or painted words and poems, leads you to believe you had entered a secret, almost forbidden world.

Public Art

In the pursuit of a personal dream or obsession, whether this is religious or secular, and with no patron, the naïve artist often ends up incorporating an aspect of mystery or fantasy in his/her creation. This is very different from the artist or group of artists working in an urban situation and expressing a social or political belief on behalf of a whole community.

A network of community artists developed during the 1970s, working in the public arena as mural painters or mosaicists to expose political or social deficiencies, to express grievances, or to promulgate ideals. The medium of mosaic, with its striking and colourful surfaces and the immediate recognition and accessibility of its materials, draws attention to itself and, subsequently, to its message, and can assist in easing or transforming a situation or in informing the public at large.

Many groups and organizations work within the public sector. In Brazil, for example, the artist Freda Jardim with her group of committed artists has executed public murals in Brazil, Chile, and Portugal.

In London, the group Free Form – originated in 1969 by the artists Martin Goodrich and Barbara Wheeler-Early – employs a skilled team of workers who work in multi-media to enhance the environment and benefit the community.

In 1985 the author formed a group of mosaic artists, Group 5, to work together on public projects within the city of Exeter, in the south-west of England. Fourteen murals have been completed, including school sites, public walkways, car parks, the arches beneath a railway bridge, and a community centre. The murals were created to give identity to, or to revitalize areas which had been neglected or were featureless and in need of civic attention through general maintenance, and to add a colourful, decorative surface.

The materials for the murals were mostly recycled and were principally donated by the citizens of the city. These

included tiles, broken crockery, china, *objets trouvés*, and miscellaneous items like car parts, together with more traditional mosaic glass. The work was created *in situ*, with the material cut and fixed on site and in all weathers. Each mural took from three months to two years to complete, working one to three days a week. Though not overtly political, the murals have become social testaments over the last twelve years and document, sometimes obliquely, the major happenings of the time: for example the disaster at Chernobyl and the opening of the Channel Tunnel between England and France.

The Tin Lane mural covers the façade of a community centre which plays host to a large programme of events, many of which are recorded on the building's exterior: playschool, youth club,

Above: **The Empress, card no. III, detail, Niki de St Phalle, dating from the 1980s, Giardino dei Tarocchi, Tuscany, Italy**
Queen of the Sky, motherhood and sacred magic, she sits in an enormous sphinx-like attitude, a mosaic of colour, mirror, tile and paint both on the outside and in the figure's interior which contains habitable domestic rooms.

Opposite page:
Mireille Levèsque, Speak White (2 x 3ft)
The Canadian artist and mosaicist uses the materials of her native land, calcite and tourmaline, alongside the more traditional materials of smalti and glass in this rough-hewn pyramidal land sculpture. The work emits a strength and endurance in which a timeless quality, so often apparent in mosaic, exists.

Right: **'Tin Lane' mosaic mural (detail), Exeter, England, E. M. Goodwin and Group 5, 1988**
The imagery of the mural reflects the social purpose of the building. Note in the foreground the 'Three Graces' – girls from the youth club being proffered a golden apple.

women's group, music club, over sixties, and others. The building's isolated position, half way down a lane lined with sheets of corrugated iron, had attracted vandalism and was in a bad state of neglect. The work on the mural attracted closer attention to the building, which in turn resulted in new safety night-time lighting, and security alarms, new windows and permanent general upkeep.

CONTEMPORARY WORK

The end of the twentieth century finds mosaic in a vigorous and vital position in the art world. Artists continue to work in two ways: as a means of self-expression, and as a means for creating objects of design. Sometimes the roles overlap. There is no right direction, only that of knowing and understanding the material and its potential.

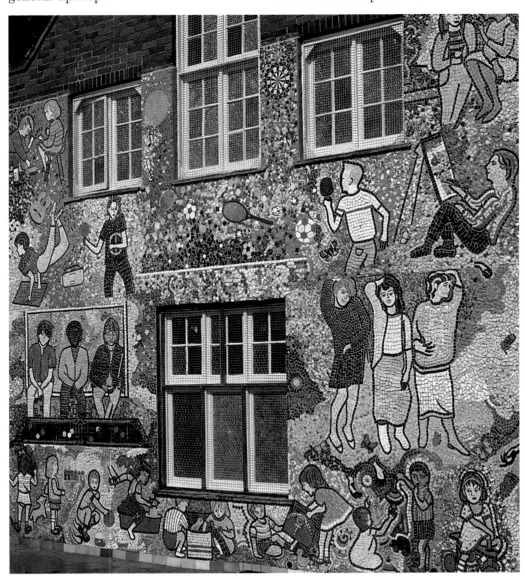

 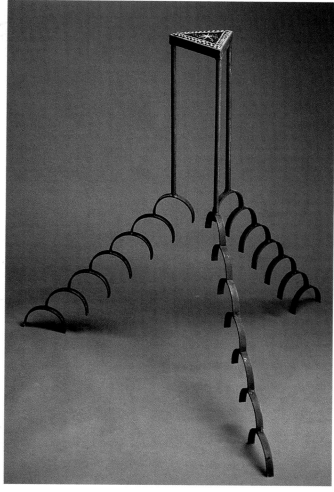

An exhibition in 1997 entitled 'Objects of Desire' took place in Ravenna, Italy; the artists were mostly Italian or Italian-trained. Some work was designed and carried out by individual artists, other objects were designed and made up by workshops specializing in translating concepts and cartoons into mosaic. The objects were an amalgam of contradiction and statement, artefacts were functional and dysfunctional, strong and forceful, elusive and whimsical, humorous and lacking any kind of comic vein. The ambiguities within their existence revealed a real examination of what an object was in a world of duplicitous standards, beliefs and ethics, and in a world of combined hopes and disillusion, creation and destruction. In an age of growing materialism, the object had become a true reflection for the end of the century, itself uncertain of what the future holds.

Worldwide, artists, with or without patrons, are investing their time, their beliefs and their creative talent into the historic medium of mosaic making. The list is impressive, and includes members of the International Association of Contemporary Mosaic Artists (Associazione Internazionale

Right: **Lucio Orsoni, Black and Blue Gold (140 x 140cm)**
The Venetian artist Lucio Orsoni makes controlled play of the sumptuous materials of Byzantium: gold and smalti.
The apex of the work holds an area of intense movement and interest within a lower geometry of illusion, linking the ancient Romans' delight in a surface of illusion to the concepts of the present day.

Mosaicisti Contemporanei) based in Italy. In Japan are Haruya Kudo and Irie Tatsuya; in France Catherine Mandron, Verdiano Marzi, Riccardo Licata and Fernanda Tollemato; in England Jane Muir and Maggie Howarth; in Brazil Freda Jardim; in Egypt Mohamed Salem; in Israel Ilana Shafir, and in Canada Mireille Levèsque.

In America Helle Scharling; in Croatia Milun Garcevic; in Norway Harriet Backer, in Germany Lino Linossi, and in Italy Marco de Luca, Stefano Mazzotti and Diego Esposito, Athos Ongaro, Antonio Trotta, Felice Nittolo, Ascaniao Renda and Lucio Orsoni.

Excellent artists all, and diverse in subject, ideas and material, but with a common link: a knowledge of the language of mosaic and an acknowledgement of its universal appeal as a medium above all others in which to decorate and express: a true medium of mass communication, as it has been for many centuries.

12 Sites and Sources

Mosaics from the present day and back to those from ancient times can be seen in numerous countries on buildings, in museums, at excavated sites, in galleries, on floors, in underground stations and subways, on and in churches and mosques – the list appears endless and varied.

Listed below, identified by country, is a collation of mosaics, by no means comprehensive, to represent the adaptability and wide usage of the medium and to provide inspirational sources from all periods of mosaic making. (The dates refer to the mosaics.)

Algeria Timgad, 2nd century.

Czech Republic St Vitus' Cathedral, Prague, 14th century.

Cyprus Paphos, 4th century BC to 4th century AD.
The church of Angeloktistou at Kiti near Larnaca, 5th century (disputed).

Egypt The monastery of St Catherine's, Mt Sinai, 6th century.
The Graeco-Roman museum, Alexandria.

England British Museum, London; Roman, Mexican, Ancient.
Kingston-upon-Hull City museum, 4th century.
Fishbourne Roman Palace, Sussex, 1st-3rd centuries.
Taunton Museum, Somerset, 4th century.
Church of St Mary and St Nicolas, Wilton, Wiltshire, mid-19th century.
St Paul's Cathedral, London, 1870–1920s.
Boris Anrep, The National Gallery, 1928–1952.
Hans Unger and Eberhard Schulze, St Judas's Church, Wigan, 1965.
Albert Memorial, Kensington, London, 1860s.
Westminster Cathedral, Victoria, London, early-mid 20th century.
Frank Brangwen, Church of St Aidan's, Harehills, Leeds, 1914–16.
Eduardo Paolozzi, Tottenham Court Road Underground, London, 1970s.

France The Louvre, Paris, Ancient, Roman.
Le Palais Idéal du Facteur Cheval, Hauterives, Drôme, 1879–1912.
F. Léger, N. D. de Toute Grace, Plateau d'Assy, Haute-Savoie, 1937–50.
Jean Bazaine, UNESCO House, Paris, 1958.
Musée de Fernand Léger, Biot, Alpes-Maritimes, 1954.
Tomb of Nureyev, Russian Cemetery, St Geneviève sous Bois, Paris, 1980s.

Germany Rheinsiches Landesmuseum, Trier.
Heinz Mack, Frankfurt am Main, Dresner Bank, 1980s.
Nennig, Saarbrücken, 2nd–4th centuries.

Greece Pella, Macedonia, 4th century BC.
Nea Moni, Chios, 11th century.
Churches of St George and Hosios David, Thessaloniki, 5th century.
Church of the monastery of Hosios Loukas, 11th century.
The island of Delos, 2nd century BC.

Above: **Collodi mosaic (Pinocchio) by Ventorino Venturi (detail)**
Childrens' theme park based on the story of Pinnochio at Collodi, Italy.

Opposite page: **Greek boat, Tavern, by Elaine M. Goodwin, 1997, Exeter, England**
An external panel evoking the colour and light of the Grecian sea.

Italy Ostia Antica, 2nd-3rd centuries AD.
Basilica and Museum of Archaeology, Aquileia, 1st century BC–3rd century AD.
Herculaneum, 1st century.
Chapel of S. Aquilino, Milan, 4th century.
Mausoleum of Galla Placidia, Ravenna, 5th century.
Church of San Vitale, Ravenna, 6th century.
St Apollinare in Classe, Ravenna, 6th century.
National Museum of Ravenna.
S. Prassede, Rome, 9th century.
S.Clemente, Rome, 12th century.
Cathedral of Monreale, Sicily, 12th century.
The basilica of SS. Maria e Donato, Murano, Venice, 12th century.
Cathedral of S. Marco Venice, 11th–15th centuries.
Parco della Pace, Ravenna, 1980s.

Jordan Archaeological museum and sites, Madaba, 5th–8th centuries.
Museum and sites, Mount Nebo, 5th–8th centuries.
Archaeological museum and sites, Jerash, 2nd–7th centuries.

Israel/Palestine Dome of the Rock mosque, Jerusalem, 7th century.
Hammath Tiberius, 6th century.
Khirbet-el-Mafjar, Jericho, 8th century.
Synagogue, Gaza, 6th century.
Synagogue of Beth Alpha, 6th century.

Lebanon Beit el Din Palace, near Beirut, 6th century.

Libya Roman Villa, Zliten, 2nd century AD.

Syria The Great Mosque, Damascus, 8th century.

Turkey Villa of Constantine, Antioch (capital of Roman Syria), 2nd century.
The Great Palace, Istanbul, 6th century.
Haghia Sophia, Istanbul, 6–12th century.
The Kariye/Chora Museum, 11th–14th centuries.

Tunisia The Bardo Museum, Tunis, 2nd–6th centuries.
Archaeological museum and sites, El Djem, 2nd century.

Morocco Site of Volubilis, near Moulay Idris, 2nd century.

Portugal Conimbrega, near Coimbra, 3rd century.

Spain Antonio Gaudí Sagrada Familia Church, and Parc Güell,
Barcelona, early 20th century.
Mihrab in the mosque/cathedral, Cordova, Andalusia, 10th century.
Ampurias, 1st–3rd centuries.

Sweden Einar Forseth, Stockholm City Hall, 1920s.

Russia St Petersburg, Cathedral of St Isaac, 19th century.
S. Sophia, Kiev, 11th century.

Stockists / Suppliers, Schools of Mosaics and Workshops

Many materials used in the art of mosaic making can be bought at art suppliers, builders' yards, hardware stores, gardencentres, tile shops and DIY shops. Specialist tools and materials coveredin this book can be obtained from thesources listed below.

Enquiries to do with mosaic-related subjects generally, and with summer schools, workshops and suppliers, can be obtained from *Mosaic Matters*, a regularly updated twice-yearly newsletter and on-line information service. Details are given at the end of this section.

United Kingdom

Reed Harris
Riverside House
27 Carnwath Road
London SW6 3HR
tel. (+44) (0)20 77 36 75 11
fax (+44) (0)20 77 36 29 88
www.reedharris.co.uk

Reed Harris
Sergeants Industrial Estate
102 Garatt Lane
London SW18 4DJ
tel. (+44) (0)20 88 77 97 74
fax (+44) (0)20 88 77 97 74
The Wandsworth showroom is specifically for mosaics

Pearsons Glass
www.pearsonsglass.com
Vitreous glass, glazed and unglazed tiles, ceramic tiles, tools, cement, cement pigment, marble, slate, sealants, mosaic nippers, tile cutters, accessories.

Edgar Udny & Co. Ltd
The Mosaic Centre
314 Balham High Road
London SW17 7AA
tel. (+44) (0)20 87 67 81 81
fax (+44) (0)20 87 67 77 09
Vitreous glass, smalti, ceramic, gold-leaf glass, tools, mosaic nippers, accessories.

Alec Tiranti Ltd
27 Warren Street
London W1P 5DG
tel/fax (+44) (0)20 73 80 08 08
also at
3 Pipers Court
Berkshire Drive
Thatcham
Berkshire RG19 4ER
tel. (+44) (0)845 123 2100
fax (+44) (0)845 123 2101
www.tiranti.co.uk
Scrim, sealer/varnish, gold and metal leaf, pigments, epoxy resin, armatures.

Opposite page:
Classroom of the School of Mosaic, Spilimbergo, Friuli, Italy, 1997

Silverland Stone
Holloway Hill
Chertsey
Kent KT16 OAE
tel. (+44) 01932 569 277
fax (+44)01932 563 558
www.silverlandstone.co.uk
Black and white pebbles.

Fothergill Engineered Fabrics Ltd
P.O. Box 1
Summit
Littleborough
Lancashire OL15 OLU
tel (+44) 01706 372 414
fax (+44) 01706 376 422
www.fothergill.co.uk
Fibre netting

Buckland Books
Holly Tree House
18 Woodlands Road
Littlehampton
West Sussex BN17 5PP
tel/fax (+44) 01903 717 648
www.bucklandbooks.co.uk
Specialist mosaic bookstore.

Italy

Angelo Orsoni snc
Cannaregio 1045
30121
Venezia
tel (+39) 041 244 0003
fax (+39) 041 524 0736
Smalti, gold, hammer (martellina),
hardie (tagliolo), mosaic nippers
(tenaglia).

Mosaici Donà Murano di Donà Stefano
Fond.ta Venier 38/a
30141 Murano (VE)
tel (+39) 041 736 596
fax (+39) 041 739 969
www.mosaicidonamurano.com
Smalti; transparent and opaque.

Mario Donà e Figli snc
Via Marchetti
4-6 Zona Artigianale
1-33097 Spilimbergo (PN)
tel/fax (+39) 0427 51125
www.donamosaici.it
Smalti.

Ferrari & Bacci snc
Via Aurelia 14
1-55045 Pietrasanta (LU)
tel (+39) 0584 790 147
fax (+39) 0584 794 182
Marble.

Mexico

Mosaicos Venecianos de Mexico SA
Cuernavaca-Cuautla Km 3.5
CP 62570 Cuernavaca
Morelos
tel. (+777) 320 2167, 320 2586
fax (+777) 320 1926, 320 4297
www.kolorines.com
UK importers for above
Wellington Tile Company
Tont Estate
Milverton Road
Wellington
Somerset TA21 OA2
www.wellingtontile.co.uk
tel (+44) 01823 667 242
fax (+44) 01823 665 685

France

Opio Colour
4 Route de Cannes
06650 OPIO
tel. (+33) 04 93 77 23 30
fax (+33) 04 93 77 40 56
Vitreous glass.

United States of America

Aqua Mix Inc
13001 Seal Beach Blvd
Seal Beach
CA 90740
tel. (+1) 800-272-8786
fax (+1) 951-256-3060
www.aquamix.com

Australia

Alan Patrick Pty Ltd
11 Agnes Steet
Jolimont
Victoria 3002
tel (+61) 03 9654 8288
fax (+61) 03 9650 5650
Vitreous, smalti, tools, accessories.

Glass Craft Australia
12 Charnfield Court
Thomastown
Northern Melbourne
Victoria 3074
tel. (+61) 03 9463 0620
fax (+61) 03 9464 1165
www.glasscraft.com.au
Vitreous glass, tools, accessories.

Schools and Institutes

Scuola Mosaicisti del Friuli (founded 1922)
Via Corridoni 6
33097 Spilimbergo
Friuli
tel. (+39) 0427 2077
fax (+39) 0427 3903
Three-year course covering all aspects of mosaicmaking.

Accademia di Belli Arti di Ravenna (founded 1827)
Via Roma 13
Loggetta Lombardesca
48100 Ravenna
tel. (+39) 514 213 641
fax (+39) 514 303 78
Four-year course in mosaic art.

Workshops

Mosaic Workshop
UnitB
443-449 Holloway Road
London N7 6LJ
tel/fax (+44) (0)20 72 72 24 46
www.mymosaicworkshop.co.uk
(founded by Emma Biggs and Tessa Hunkin, 1988)
Mosaic kits, restoration, commissions, stockist, workshops.

Akomena Spazio Mosaico
Via Roma 58/60
48100 Ravenna
tel/fax (+39) 0544 37119
(founded by Francesca Fabbri, 1988)
Experimental and contemporary workshop.

Bibliography

ARGAN, G. C., et al., *Mosaico d'Amicizia fra i Popoli: Parco Della Pace Ravenna*, Longo Editore, 1988.

AVI-YONAH, Michael, *Ancient Mosaics*, Cassell, 1975.

AYYILDIZ, Ugur, *Chora: the Kariye Museum*, Net Turistik Yayinlar a.s., 1993.

BEN DOV, Meir, and Yoel Rappel, *Mosaics of the Holy Land*, Adama Books, 1987.

BERTELLI, Carlo, *Il Mosaico*, Arnoldo Mondadori, 1988.

BLANCHARD-LEMÉE, M. et al., *Mosaics of Roman Africa*, British Museum Press, 1996.

BOVINI, Giuseppe, *Ravenna, Art and History*, Longo Editore, 1991.

CLARKE, John R., *Roman Black and White Figural Mosaics*, New York University Press, 1979.

DEMUS, Otto, *The Mosaic Decoration of San Marco, Venice*, University of Chicago Press, 1988.

DONNER, Herbert, *The Mosaic Map of Madaba*, Kok Pharos Publishing House, 1992.

DUCREY, Pierre, *Eretria*, Swiss School of Archaeology, Athens, 1991.

FARNETI, Manuela, *Glossario Tecnico-Storico del Mosaico*, Longo Editore, 1993.

FISCHER, P, *Mosaic: History and Technique*, Thames and Hudson, 1971.

FIELD, Robert, *Geometric Patterns from Roman Mosaics, and How to Draw Them*, Tarquin Publications, 1988, 2nd ed.1996.

GOLDSTONE, Bud, and Arloa Paquin Goldstone, *The Los Angeles Watts Towers*, Thames and Hudson, 1997.

GOODWIN, Elaine M., *Classic Mosaic*, Apple Books.

GOODWIN, Elaine M., *Decorative Mosaics*, Letts/New Holland, 1992.

HARVEY, Hazel, *Discovering Exeter: Community Mosaics*, Exeter Civic Society, 1998.

ITTEN, Johannes, *The Elements of Colour*, Van Nostrand Reinhold Co., 1970.

JOHNSON, Peter, *Romano-British Mosaics*, Shire Publications Ltd., 1982.

L'ORANGE, H. P. and P. J. Nordhagen, *Mosaics: From Antiquity to the Early Middle Ages*, Methuen and Co., 1966.

MASCHERPA, Giorgio, *Severini e il Mosaico*, Angelo Longo Editore, 1985.

MOLDI RAVENNA, Cristiana, *I Colori della Luce: Angelo Orsoni e l'Arte del Mosaico*, Marsilio Editore, 1996.

MORHANGE, Angelina, *Boris Anrep: the National Gallery Mosaics*, The National Gallery London, 1979.

PEGORARO, Silvia, *Oggetti del Desiderio*, Electa, 1991.

PICCIRILLO, Michele, *The Mosaics of Jordan*, The American Center of Oriental Research, 1993.

ROCHFORT, Desmond, *Mexican Muralists*, Laurence King Publishing, 1997.

ROSSI, Ferdinando, *Mosaics: A Survey of their History and Techniques*, Pall Mall Press, 1970.

SAINT PHALLE, Niki de, *The Tarot Garden*, Benteli, 1997.

SAKELLARAKI, Efi Saouna, Eretria, Ministry of Culture, Archeological Receipts Fund, 1995.

SMITH, D. J., *Roman Mosaics at Hull*, City of Hull Museums & Art Galleries, 1987.

UNGER, Hans, *Practical Mosaics*, Studio Vista, 1965.

Glossary

aggregate Granular material made from broken stones, bricks and pebbles, used in making concrete.

amazonomachia Representation of female fighters battling warrior women; a favourite subject of Greek artists (mythical Amazons).

ambulatory Arcade, passage or aisle, usually in an apse or cloister.

andamento Movement or coursing of tesserae, also the flow of the grout lines.

apse Semi-circular, arched or domed end to a building. In a church this is generally the east end.

arabesque Delicate flowing forms ending in scrolls and decorated with leaves or flowers.

armature Wire framework giving base support for a three dimensional work.

asaroton/os The 'unswept floor' mosaics, depicting in a random and scattered manner debris and leavings from the table.

Bacchantes, or Maenads Female worshippers of the god of wine: Dionysus (Greek); Bacchus (Roman).

baptistry Also called the illuminatorium. A separate or integral part of a church used for the baptismal rite.

basilica Rectangular building often with an apsidal end, adapted from the Roman design into the Christian church, with added aisles and nave.

calcination Process of burning lime and clay at very high temperatures (c. 1500°C) and reducing the resulting residue or clinker to a finely ground grey cement powder.

cantharus Wide-mouthed drinking cup or vase with a foot and two handles.

cement Substance made by calcining lime and clay. Used as a binder or mortar.

ceramic Used to describe all products made from clay.

chiaroscuro Italian for 'light/dark'. The treatment of light and shade in an art work.

Chi-rho or Christogram Monogram of Christ, made by the first two letters of the Greek 'Christos' – chi rho.

cithara Early musical instrument with strings and a sounding board, the precursor of the lute, cithern, zither and guitar.

conté crayon Unique French drawing stick which is grease-free.

countersink Bevelling of the edge of a hole as for a screw-head, made by a countersink tool or bit.

De Stijl The Style: a Dutch artistic movement of 1917–1928, whose proponents were uncompromisingly abstract in their work, often using the primary colours, red, blue and yellow.

Dionysus/os God of the vine; widely worshipped as a symbol of death and renewal of vegetation.

emblema/ta Central mosaic panel(s), often prefabricated and of fine workmanship made up on a marble or terracotta tray away from site.

fauces Narrow, oblong space, threshold or entry way.

fool's gold Iron pyrites; lustrous yellow-coloured iron sulphide material.

gnomon Rod or pin of a dial, whose shadow points to the hours.

grid Symmetrical system of patterning commonly made of rectangles or squares.

guilloche Linear pattern in the form of an entwined plait or braid of two or more strands.

icon Image or sacred work.

iconography The art of illustration.

lozenge Diamond or rhomboid shape.

meander Continuous all-over winding patterning.

mihrab Niche, usually in a religious building, indicating the direction of Mecca and therefore prayer.

mortar Mix of sand, (lime) cement, and water.

nereid Sea nymph.

Nilotic Pertaining to the River Nile in Egypt and its environs; encompassing imagery of the lotus, geese and ducks.

nimbus Halo, disc or aureole which circles the head of a divine, sacred or ideal personage.

nymphaeum/aea Groves or grottoes sacred to the nymphs or lesser female divinities and guardian spirits.

nucleus In classical pavements; the penultimate layer in a setting bed or foundation.

objets trouvés Found objects.

officina/e Mosaic workshop or school.

Pantocrator The creator of all; the Almighty, universal judge.

pattern Arrangement of decorative motifs

pattern book Collection of designs, motifs and patterns used by mosaicists.

pelta Semi-circular shield, stylized in Roman art.

pictor imaginarius Master mosaicist.

plasticizer Additive which promotes elasticity or pliability.

reinforced concrete Concrete strengthened by embedded metal or wire.

rudus Classical term used to describe the second or intermediary layer, in a setting bed or foundation.

scrim Loosely woven fabric or gauze.

setting bed Base or foundation onto which a mosaic is laid; the substratum beneath the piece.

sfumato (Italian): 'smoke'. An almost imperceptible transition of colour change in tone or value.

slurry Mix of cement mortar with water added to give it a runny consistency.

soffit Underside of an arch or lintel.

spandrel Triangular-shaped space formed between arches and often decorated.

spatula Tool of plastic, wood or metal used for mixing or spreading.

statumen Classical term for the base level of a setting bed or foundation.

terracotta Clay baked to a high temperature, ranging in colour from orange to brown.

tessera/ae Also tessella. A cube-shaped piece of stone or other material used to make a mosaic.

tesserula/ae Diminutive tesserae.

therme/ae Roman baths.

triclinium Roman dining room, particularly designed for three couches.

trompe l'oeil Design to 'deceive the eye' and appear as if real.

xenia From the Greek word for 'hospitality'; floors whose Imagery depicts great abundance.

PHOTO CREDITS

The author and the publisher wish to thank the following for their kind permission to reproduce the photographs in this book.
Garth Blore, p.22
Kingston upon Hull City Museums, East Yorkshire, England, p.87
The Mosaics of Jordan by Michele Piccirillo, 1993, pub. American Center of Oriental Research, Amman, Jordan, pp.90,91
Severini e il Mosaico by G. Mascherpa, 1985, pub. Longo Editore, Ravenna, Italy, p.107
Ugo Marano, Cetara, Italy, p.113
Mireille Levesque, Quebec, Canada, p.113
Lucio Orsoni, Venice, Italy, p.114
Elaine M. Goodwin, pp.10,27,36,68,70, 80,82,83,88,89,92,93,94,97,99,100,102, 103,105,106,108,109,110,111,112,116,118
All other photos by John Melville, Exeter, England.

USEFUL INFORMATION

Mosaic Matters was initiated in 1991 by Elaine M. Goodwin and Paul Bentley as a twice-yearly publication, and is one of the oldest newsletters on the subject. It went electronic in 1997, and is now entirely web-based, still edited by Paul Bentley and maintained by its webmaster Andy Mitchell. The website is regularly updated and includes details of courses, new publications, exhibitions, and so on, as well as illustrated articles of more general interest and a section for questions, answers and exchange of information. It can be found at www.mosaicmatters.co.uk.

Index